Schriften zur
Europäischen Integration und
Internationalen Wirtschaftsordnung

Veröffentlichungen des
Wilhelm Merton-Zentrums für Europäische Integration und
Internationale Wirtschaftsordnung,

herausgegeben von

Professor Dr. Dr. Rainer Hofmann, Universität Frankfurt a. M.
Professor Dr. Stefan Kadelbach, Universität Frankfurt a. M.
Professor Dr. Rainer Klump, Universität Frankfurt a. M.

Band 29

Cordula Rutz/Prof. Dr. Rainer Klump/Jörg Schramek
Prof. Dr. Winfried von Urff (eds.)

Synthesis and assessment of the public debate on the reform of the CAP after 2013

Nomos

Gedruckt mit freundlicher Unterstützung der Landwirtschaftlichen Rentenbank, Frankfurt am Main.

Die Deutsche Nationalbibliothek lists this publication in the Deutsche Nationalbibliografie; detailed bibliographic data is available in the Internet at http://dnb.d-nb.de.

ISBN 978-3-8487-0172-8

1. Edition 2013

Preface

The European Union is currently going through one of the severe – some observers say even the most severe – period of its history. The Euro crisis which originated from unsolved problems with public indebtedness in various EU member countries risks undermining also the foundations on which the Common Market has been built over the last 60 years. In these times of crisis it is important to remember that none of the achievements which the Europeans were able to realize within only a few decades could be taken for granted at the beginning. Each step for further integration has usually not been easy to go, as at lot of different interests of various stakeholders in the different member countries bringing up a multitude of different cost-benefit ratios have to be balanced.

In this context it is worth remembering that from its beginnings in the 1950 s up to now the Common Agricultural Policy (CAP) has been an important element of joint interest for all European countries. After two terrible world wars in the first half of the century and confronted with the dissolution of the former colonial empires all countries in Europe were faced with enormous problems of how to guarantee the stable and sufficient food supply of their citizens. Hence the higher efficiency and higher output of domestic food production became one of the basic economic as well as political goals of CAP, for which the member countries were also willing to pay a price. Even if the goal of self-sufficiency could be achieved by the beginning of the 1970 s and has been more and more amended by other political goals, such as sustainable Management of natural resources or balanced regional development, it still plays and will play a significant role, in particular in times of rising international crises. Despite the relatively high budget which the Union spends every year for CAP there seems to be rare unanimity that the common responsibility for agriculture is and will be one of the cornerstones of European integration.

2013 will be a decisive year not only for the Euro, but also for the future course of CAP. In 2010 with its Communication the European Communication has invited a broad debate all over Europe on the future goals and policy options of CAP after 2013. The Commission's Communication has also been the starting point of our research project which aims at a synthesis of the discussions in ten member countries being more or less representative of the whole Union. We were able to bring together statements from various stakeholders in the future development of CAP, ranging from government officials to NGOs and agricultural economists and condense them into country reports. These reports become the source for a synthesis which was intensively discussed at the occasion of an international conference at Goethe-University Frankfurt am Main in March 2012. The final version of this synthesis goes now public with this book. Even if not all relevant positions might be covered the final synthesis certainly documents the most important arguments in the discussions which will accompany the next step of CAP, including the decisions on the necessary financial frame.

A multi-facetted research project like this one would not be feasible without many reliable collaborators for whose support and contributions I am extremely grateful. My sincere thanks go to Cordula Rutz, Jörg Schramek and Winfried von Urff from Institut für Ländliche Strukturforschung (Ifls) in Frankfurt am Main for the excellent work in organizing the country reports and compiling the synthesis as well as in co-organizing the international conference "Is the Common Agricultural Policy rising to its challenges? A European Dialogue". This conference brought together experts from 14 EU member states and gave them a forum for vivid debates and discussions. Also, I would like to thank Landwirtschaftliche Rentenbank, Frankfurt am Main, for its generous support of this research project. Finally, my thanks go to Patrick Messerlin and the team members of Group Economie Mondiale (GEM) at Sciences Po, Paris, for the cooperation and the hospitality during the preparation of parts of the project, and to Inga Buschmann, in particular for handling the publication process of this volume.

Frankfurt am Main, October 2012 Prof. Dr. Rainer Klump

Table of Contents

List of Figures

List of Tables

List of Abbreviations

CAP:	Common Agricultural Policy
EC	European Commission
EU	European Union
EAFRD	European Agricultural Fund for Rural Development
EAGF	European Agricultural Guarantee Fund
GATT	General Agreement on Tariffs and Trade
GDP	Gross domestic product
LAG	Local Action Group
LEADER	Liaison Entre Actions de Développement de l'Économie Rurale
LFA	Less-favoured area
NGO	Non-governmental organisation
SAPS	Single Area Payment Scheme
SPS	Single Payment Scheme

1 Executive Summary

The EU Common Agricultural Policy (CAP) has undergone several reform processes since its creation after World War II. The concepts of multifunctionality of farming and sustainability have gained importance, rural development policies have become part of the CAP and environmental concerns are targeted via binding obligations as well as optional agri-environmental measures. Over the years, the CAP has moved more and more away from price support mechanisms to direct payments. An important reform step was the decoupling of direct payments from production in the so-called Fischler reform of 2003. However, amongst other things, the degree of decoupling and the system of implementation of direct payments vary between the Member States. Also, different stakeholder groups take different views on what the objectives of a European agricultural policy should be and what instruments should be applied in order to meet these objectives. These different views become evident in the public debate on the reform of the CAP after 2013.

The **aim of this research project** was to summarise and asses the public debate on the reform of the CAP after 2013 in ten EU Member States following the publication of the European Commissions' Communication entitled "The CAP towards 2020: Meeting the food, natural resources and territorial challenges of the future" (COM 2010 672 final) in November 2010. In this Communication the Commission describes the previous reform path of the CAP, defines future challenges for the CAP (food security, environment and climate change, territorial balance) sets out objectives of the future CAP (viable food production, sustainable management of natural resources and climate action, balanced territorial development) and specifies future instruments (including the capping and greening of direct payments)[1] as well as three broad policy options (EC 2010 a).

For the purpose of this analysis various statements of stakeholders in the public debate on agricultural policy, like governments, farmers' unions, scientists or environmental non-governmental organisations were analysed by country experts in the Czech Republic, Finland, France, Germany, the United Kingdom (UK), Greece, Hungary, Poland, Slovenia and Spain. The selected Member States represent new as well as old Member States and a variety of climatic conditions and agricultural structures.

1 A summary of the Commission's proposals as expressed in the Communication of November 2010 and the Legal Proposals of October 2011 is provided in chapter 3.

In their reports the experts summarised the stakeholders' positions on the different elements of the CAP reform proposed in the Commission's Communication, put them into context, determined the issues dominating the debate in the respective Member State and drew conclusions. Reactions of stakeholders towards the far more detailed legal proposals published by the EU Commission in October 2011 could only be included in the reports if they were accessible at time of writing (September until end of October 2011). So, even if reactions to the legal proposals were incorporated as far as possible, most of the analysed statements refer to the Communication of November 2010.

The country reports provided the basis of the **synthesis report**. It is in the nature of such a synthesis that it cannot reflect the whole range of opinions contained in the country reports. The authors tried to identify main lines of argument, common aspects and differences in and between the public debates in the analysed countries. Even though this was done with all due care, it cannot be ruled out that that the relative importance of certain aspects is assessed differently by those who participated in the debate. It must also be noted that as the debate on the future CAP is still ongoing and very dynamic the results presented here must be seen as a snapshot of the debate in the weeks following the publication of the reform proposals.

The synthesis report formed the basis for discussion at an international conference in March 2012.

The **stakeholders mainly involved** in the public debate in the ten analysed Member States are:

- Governmental bodies: Mostly, the ministries of agriculture elaborate the national governments' position on the CAP reform. Sometimes the ministries of the environment or governmental environmental agencies prepare their own statements, which can, like in the case of France, differ substantially from the position taken by the ministry of agriculture. In some countries, like Spain, Germany and the UK, regional administrative agencies also draw up their own, sometimes diverging, positions.
- Farmers' unions, land owners' associations, associations of agricultural cooperatives.
- Non-governmental organisations (NGOs) in the fields of environmental protection and nature conservation, development cooperation and rural development: their involvement differs in scale and scope from Member State to Member State, e.g. some NGOs in Germany make quite detailed suggestions (for example with regard to the greening of direct payments), whereas NGOs in Finland publish more general statements about agriculture.
- Scientific councils and think tanks.

Apart from the overall objectives and the general architecture of the CAP, the **issues dominating** the debate on the CAP reform in the ten analysed Member States are:[2]

- The proposed greening of direct payments.
- The capping of direct payments: mainly discussed in those Member States where some large farms might be affected by such a policy, such as the Czech Republic or Germany.
- The limiting of support to "active farmers" and the respective definition of the term.
- The harmonisation of direct payments schemes in the EU, the degree of decoupling and the way to implement decoupled direct payments.
- The call for a simplification of the CAP and a reduction of bureaucracy.
- The overall scale of the CAP funding.
- The distribution of funds between Member States: the call for a more equitable distribution of funds between new and old Member States is the dominating issue in most new Member States.
- The wish to maintain agricultural production in the entire EU and to ensure sufficient income for farmers.
- Market measures: a focus of the debate in some countries, like Spain and France, while of minor importance in other countries, e.g. Slovenia.
- Issues of specific national interest, e.g. national support to certain sectors or areas.
- Rural development policies: of interest in some, mainly new, Member States and of hardly any importance in other Member States, e.g. France. In some countries, like Germany, the debate on rural development only gathered momentum after the publication of the legal proposals in October 2011 and therefore could only partially be reflected in this study.

Challenges and Targets

Most stakeholders agree in principal with the **challenges and targets** identified by the Commission. However, different groups of stakeholders stress different challenges and objectives. For many governments alongside with the mainstream farming organisations competitiveness and productivity (often seen in connection with the need to contribute to global food security) of the EU farming sector should be the main objectives of the CAP. Neither governments (with the exemption of the UK central government, which calls for a shift from a policy of support for the agricultural sector as such to a policy of public support for the provisions of public goods) nor the mainstream farming organisations demand a **fundamental re-**

2 The order of the issues listed is not weighted.

form of the CAP. A fundamental reform is often demanded by agricultural economists and NGOs. However, while environmental and other NGOs, like scientists, frequently demand a more fundamental reform and improved targeting of the CAP they often favour strict environmental and social regulations both in the EU and with regard to international agricultural trade over market liberalisation.

Reform Orientation

The **two-pillar structure** of the CAP is hardly questioned by governmental bodies in the analysed countries. Only the UK central government argues in favour of phasing out the first pillar for the benefit of a strengthened second pillar. The mainstream farming organisations also accept the current two-pillar structure, but often state that pillar two must not be strengthened at the expense of pillar one. Like most governmental bodies, the farming organisations would like to see the two pillars to be kept distinctly divided. In the opinion of most mainstream farming organisations the focus of the second pillar should lie on support to the agricultural sector, but the opinions range from the Polish agricultural chamber, which explicitly acknowledges the importance of the rural development measures of the CAP, to some farmers' organisations in Spain that would like to see rural development policies to be excluded from the CAP and to become part of cohesion policies. Various proposals to change the current structure of the CAP come from scientific bodies and NGOs.

With regard to the **funding** of the CAP only the UK central government and some scientists call for a drastic reduction of the overall EU CAP budget. Most governments, alongside with the farming organisations and NGOs argue in favour of a financially strong CAP. Especially the new Member States oppose any suggestion to increase the burden on national budgets or in their words to "renationalise" the agricultural policy. They, like the farmers' organisations in the new Member States, strongly demand a **more equitable distribution** of funds, especially with regard to direct payments, between the old and new Member States. This claim is more or less openly rejected by the governments and farming organisations in the old Member States, which argue that only a minor redistribution would be acceptable in order to avoid disruptions and that the distribution of funds should be based on criteria such as the contribution of a country to the EU budget or that differences in purchasing power and production costs should be taken into account.

Direct Payments

Interestingly, not all governments of the countries included in this analysis, had yet publicly expressed a position on the proposed **capping of direct payments** received per farm. The opponents, the Czech Republic, the German federal government and the UK central government argue that such a policy would impair competitiveness and increase bureaucracy. The German federal government additionally argues that direct payments serve as remuneration for public goods provided per hectare by small and large farms alike. The Hungarian government attaches its support to the condition that the remaining funds can be used according to national priorities. Some governmental and administrative bodies in France suggest a distribution based on employment. The mainstream farmers' organisations, which take a position on this issue, mainly oppose it as having a negative impact on efficiency and impairing necessary structural change. However, farming organisations in Greece, like the Greek government, support such a policy, just like NGOs from all countries which also support the coupling of the provision of direct payments with employment. The proposal to limit the provision of direct payments to **"active farmers"** is opposed by a number of governments, either on the grounds that such a policy would have adverse effects on part-time farmers or on the grounds that the implementation should be optional for Member States. However, even the governments as well as the farmers' organisations that support such a policy in principle, criticise the proposed definition of "active farmer", either as too wide or as too narrow. Non-governmental organisations disagree on that issue. While some, e.g. environmental and social initiatives in Poland, support the limitation to "active farmers", others, like environmental organisations in Spain, argue that support should be granted to all "good stewards".

With regard to the **greening of direct payments** many governments, like the ones of Greece, Poland or Spain, argue that such a policy would constitute an additional burden on farmers, create additional costs and therefore impair the competitiveness of the EU agricultural sector. This opinion is in line with the view of the mainstream agricultural organisations, which mostly fiercely oppose the introduction of 7% ecological focus areas as this is seen as counterproductive in times of rising demand for food and biomass for energy production. Other governments, like in Slovenia, principally accept the proposal, but argue that the specifications are too rigid or should be adapted to national conditions. The UK central government questions the environmental benefits of such a policy. Scientists from different countries mostly argue in favour of an implementation of environmental policies via the second pillar in the form of contractual payments. The intention of the greening is very much supported by most NGOs, but, especially after the concrete obligations were made public, many expressed their disappointment as the obligations are seen as insufficient or even counterproductive.

In many countries, such as Spain, France and Finland governments would like to furthermore be able to support at least certain sectors of national interest with

coupled payments. In Hungary, Greece, Slovenia and Poland additional support to **small farms** is regarded necessary.

Market Measures

With regard to market measures most governments support the introduction of additional **risk management tools**, only the UK central government stresses that this should be in the form of temporary support to private instruments. Such a temporary form of support is also brought forward by scientists from France, and Germany. NGOs from Germany criticise the concept of supported risk insurances as this is seen to favour risky input-intensive high-yielding production methods and provide a disincentive for farmers to adopt precautionary measures. Proposals to strengthen the **role of producers** in the food supply chain are broadly welcomed by governments as well as by farming organisations. Opinions on **supply management and intervention mechanisms** differ widely. Some countries, like Spain and France emphasise the importance of supply management tools and intervention systems. Others, like the Slovenian government, which supports the abolishment of the sugar quota system, but would like to keep up the existing system of wine planting rights, take a middle position. The UK central government argues in favour of a simplified system of market measures and would like to see all quota systems to be abolished. This position is in line with the view of scientists from several countries, some of whom also emphasise the need to foster quality production. The abolishment of **export subsidies** is demanded by the UK central government, the federal government of Germany (under WTO rules) as well as scientists and NGOs from several countries. An issue put forward by many non-governmental organisations is the demand to support **local food markets**. NGOs from France and Spain, like their national and regional governments (and in the case of Spain also like the farmers' unions), call for **stricter environmental and social rules** to be applied to imported food.

Rural Development

Different opinions prevail on the question what the focus of the second pillar should be. While mainly the mainstream farming organisations and some governmental bodies, like in Spain, argue that the focus should lie on agriculture and its competitiveness, others, like governmental bodies, scientists and NGOs from Poland, Hungary, Germany and the UK stress the importance of **integrated rural development** measures and would like to see the **LEADER** approach to be strengthened in the future rural development policy. The need to ensure that an adequate share of second pillar funds is spent on **environmental measures** is stressed by NGOs from several countries.

Some stakeholders, like governmental bodies, scientists and NGOs from Finland, welcome the idea to base compensatory payments on **biophysical and/or climatic criteria**, although it has to be noted that only few of the analysed stakeholders expressed an opinion on that topic. Others, e.g. governmental bodies and the mainstream farming organisations oppose or at least question the approach. Better **targeting** of second pillar funds in general as well as the simplification of the monitoring and evaluation process is demanded by many stakeholders.

Conclusions from the written assessment

The range of opinions presented in this study is truly broad. At the one end of the spectrum the debate in countries like Spain or France is dominated by the call for strongly interventionists policies protecting European farmers from international competition and volatile prices, while at the other end most stakeholders in the United Kingdom try to find ways to efficiently target the public funds provided by the CAP on the provision of public goods and services.

Overall, it becomes evident that the positions adopted by the various groups of stakeholders are influenced by

- their convictions about what the objectives of the CAP should be, especially with regard to the question how the European agricultural sector and thus the CAP can best contribute to global food security,
- national characteristics, like the prevailing climatic conditions, the agricultural structure, the political and administrative system and historical developments,
- sectoral interests, e.g. with regard to the introduction of stricter environmental obligations demanded by environmental NGOs and opposed by the mainstream farmers' organisations.

Closing conference

The findings presented in the synthesis report formed the basis for discussion at an international conference which allowed scrutinising the results obtained so far. The conference was attended by approximately 120 participants from 14 European Member States. The stakeholder groups represented best were the scientific community as well as administrative bodies (on national, regional and local levels). In addition to commenting statements by representatives from different political levels on CAP reform and the synthesis report, the Commission's proposals on the greening of direct payments, the capping and the limitation of support to "active farmers" as well as the proposals for the second pillar were discussed in more detail in working groups. The greening was generally seen more positive by the participants of the conference than in the statements by the stakeholder groups compiled in the country reports. Some suggestions for improvements, which might make the greening more effective and more acceptable for farmers, were made. With regard to the capping and "active farmers" proposals the participants recognised the Commission's intention to achieve a fairer distribution of direct payments between farmers', which might improve the social acceptance of the CAP. However, the proposed measures in their current form were criticised as poorly-targeted and overly bureaucratic. Overall, it became evident that stringent and consistent decisions on the future of direct payments can only be made if the function of direct payments is clearly defined. The new design of the second pillar proposed by the Commission was seen to have positive potential (e.g. greater flexibility and multi-fund approach). However, the participants argued that in order to make use of this potential "guard rails" and further clarifications are needed.

2 Introduction

In the following sections the purpose and methodology of this research project are described followed by a brief review of previous CAP reforms and an overview of the state of implementation of the last reform steps in the Member States included in the analysis.

2.1 Purpose and Methodology of the Research Project

The publication of a Communication from the European Commission to the European Parliament, the Council, the European Economic and Social Committee and the Committee of the Regions entitled "The CAP towards 2020: Meeting the food, natural resources and territorial challenges of the future" (COM 2010 672 final) on November 18th 2010 was followed by an intensive public debate throughout the European Member States. In this Communication the Commission describes the previous reform path of the CAP, defines future challenges for the CAP (food security, environment and climate change, territorial balance) sets out objectives of the future CAP (viable food production, sustainable management of natural resources and climate action, balanced territorial development) and specifies future instruments (including the capping and greening of direct payments) as well as three broad policy options (EC 2010 a). Option 1 describes a continuation of the current policy with some adjustments regarding the distribution of direct payments between Member States. Option 2, which is clearly favoured by the Commission, aims at creating a more sustainable and better targeted CAP that contributes more to the EU 2020 strategy of smart, sustainable and inclusive growth. Option 3 describes a fundamental reform with a strong focus on environmental protection and climate action moving away from income support and market measures.

The aim of the research project was to summarise and asses the public debate on the reform of the CAP after 2013 in ten EU Member States following the publication of this Communication. For this purpose various statements of stakeholders in the public debate on agricultural policy, like governments, farmers' unions, scientists or environmental non-governmental organisations were analysed by country experts in the Czech Republic, Finland, France, Germany, the United Kingdom,

Greece, Hungary, Poland, Slovenia and Spain.[3] The selected Member States represent new as well as old Member States and a variety of climatic conditions and agricultural structures.

In the country reports the experts summarised the stakeholders' positions on the different elements of the CAP reform proposed in the Commission's Communication, put them into context, determined the issues dominating the debate in the respective Member State and drew conclusions. Reactions of stakeholders towards the far more detailed legal proposals published by the EU Commission in October 2011 could only be included in the reports if they were accessible at time of writing (September until end of October 2011). So, even if reactions to the legal proposals were incorporated as far as possible, most of the analysed statements refer to the Communication of November 2010.

The country reports provide the basis of the **synthesis report**. It is in the nature of such a synthesis that it cannot reflect the whole range of opinions contained in the country reports. The authors tried to identify main lines of argument, common aspects and differences in and between the public debates in the analysed countries. Even though this was done with all due care, it cannot be ruled out that that the relative importance of certain aspects is assessed differently by those who participated in the debate. It must also be noted that as the debate on the future CAP is still ongoing and very dynamic the results presented here must be seen as a snapshot of the debate in the weeks following the publication of the reform proposals.

The findings presented in the synthesis report formed the basis for discussion at an international conference in March 2012 under the heading "Is the CAP rising to its challenges? A European dialogue", which allowed scrutinizing the results obtained so far. In particular the following objectives were pursued:

- Critical analysis of the European Commission's proposals with regard to the future of direct payments, market measures and rural development policy instruments.
- Identification of possible compromises, but also unbridgeable differences, between the various stakeholders at the national and international level as a contribution to the process of political opinion making.

The conference was attended by roughly 120 participants from 14 EU Member States. In addition to the nations included in the analysis participants from the following countries were present: the Netherlands, Latvia, Belgium and Austria. As the conference took place in Germany most participants were German. The next biggest groups of participants came from the Netherlands, France, Spain and the UK. The stakeholder groups represented best were the scientific community as well

3 See Dwyer and Lewis 2011, Juvančič 2012, Lataste and Trouvé 2011, Liesivaara et al. 2011, Nurzyńska 2011, Ocsko 2011, Prazan 2011, Rutz et al. 2011, Viladomiu and Rosell 2011, Vlahos and Klonaris 2011.

as administrative bodies (on national, regional and local levels). While some experts from governmental environmental agencies attended, only few representatives of NGOs were present. Also, only a relatively small number of farmers' organisations were represented.

2.2 The CAP Reform Process

The following sections provide an overview of the CAP reform process in order to put the current reform step and the issues raised in the public debate into context.

2.2.1 Brief Review of Previous Reforms

The CAP, originally designed after World War II to avoid food shortages and to stabilise farm incomes, has undergone several reform steps. The need for the first reforms, like the introduction of the milk quota system in 1984, arose from the negative consequences of price support through import tariffs and intervention, namely structural overproduction and rapidly increasing costs. Additionally, conflicts with international trading partners, that became a subject of the GATT (General Agreement on Tariffs and Trade)-Uruguay-round (1986-1994) increased the pressure to reform. As a consequence prices of cereals and beef were brought closer in line with world market prices in the so-called Mac Sharry-reform in 1992. In order to compensate farmers for the resulting income loss direct payments were introduced (EP 2011 and Hofreither 2011).

Following the Cork Conference on Rural Development in 1996 the terms "sustainability" and "multifunctionality" of agriculture grew in importance leading to the endorsement of the "European Model of Agriculture" as a policy framework by the Council of Ministers (Thomson et al. 2010). The Agenda 2000 reform in 1999 continued on this reform path and introduced the development of rural areas as the second pillar of the CAP. The current EU's Rural Development Policy for the period of 2007 until 2013 focuses on three main objectives, the so-called axes, namely improving

- the competitiveness of the agricultural sector,
- the environment and the countryside,
- the quality of life in rural areas and the diversification of the rural economy.

Member States and regions must spread their funding between these three axes and some of the measures must be based on the LEADER (Liaison Entre Actions de Développement de l'Économie Rurale) approach (horizontal axis four) involving projects designed and executed by Local Action Groups (LAGs) (EC 2011 f).

The next important step in the reform was the decoupling of direct payments from production in 2003 (the so-called Fischler-reform), which also linked direct payments with compulsory environmental, food safety and animal welfare standards, the so-called cross-compliance obligations (EP 2011 and Hofreither 2011). Also, progressive modulation rates allowing a transfer from funds from pillar one, the European Agricultural Guarantee Fund (EAGF), to pillar 2, the European Agricultural Fund for Rural Development (EAFRD) were introduced (EC 2011 a). The policy shift to decoupled direct payments and to a more target-oriented policy focused on market-based activities and rural development can be seen as a radical change in the CAP. This rather radical reform step, which was originally meant to be a mere "mid-term" review of the Agenda 2000 reform, was according to Swinnen (2008) made possible by three main sets of influencing factors, namely

- the effect of institutional reforms (EU enlargement, introduction of qualified majority voting),
- the optimal conditions for reform (pressures for reform, like the WTO negotiations, budget, environmental and food safety concerns resulting in a loss of legitimacy of the CAP as well as, to a lesser extent, the Eastern enlargement) and
- changes in the number and quality of political players (increasing influence of consumer and environmental groups and less impact of farmers' unions, administrative reforms and generational changes in the Directorate-General for agriculture and the vision, tactics and experience of the Commissioner).

However, there was hardly any redistribution of funds between Member States and farmers, the reform had little effect on border protection and the shift in rhetoric with a new focus on rural development was not matched by an analogous shift of financial resources from the first to the second pillar (ibid.).

The 2003 reform allowed for some flexibility of implementation with regard to the decoupling and calculation of direct payments in the Member States. The resulting differences are explained in more detail in the following section.

Table 1 provides an overview of the major steps in the development of the CAP.

Table 1: Development of the Common Agricultural Policy

Period	Characteristics	Milestones
1960-1969	Establishment of various different common market organisations (CMOs)	– 1962: market organisations for cereals and related products – 1964: market organisations for milk and dairy products
1970-1980	When world prices declined, a strong agricultural income-oriented market and price policy was pursued. However, the product markets seemed less "manageable" than before, causing major problems of surpluses and high expenditure.	– 1972: Three directives on agriculture structure policy – 1973: Accession of United Kingdom, Ireland and Denmark – 1975: first environmental directive; Less Favoured Area Directive – 1979: Birds Directive – 1981: Accession of Greece – 1984: Introduction of milk quota – 1985: Council Regulation on improving the efficiency of agricultural structures – 1986: Accession of Portugal and Spain
1992-2003	Transformation – started by the Mac Sharry- reforms of 1992 and followed by the 1999 decisions on Agenda 2000 – to price reduction and farm income compensation, coupled to volume restrictions (set-aside obligations) and a more market-oriented approach.	– 1992: Mac Sharry-reform: from price support to direct payments; Completion of the Single European Market; Maastricht Treaty – 1994: GATT Uruguay Round Agreement on Agriculture – 1995: Accession of Austria, Sweden, Finland – 1996: BSE crisis; Cork Conference on Rural Development Policy – 1999: Agenda 2000: further shift from price support to direct payments and start of rural development policy – 2001: start of WTO Doha Development Agenda negotiations

Period	Characteristics	Milestones
2003-present	In the Fischler- and the Health Check reforms, decoupling (from current production) of direct income payments and introduction of management guidelines (cross-compliance). Export refunds substantially reduced. A single common market organisation. Market, price and farm income policy partly replaced by rural development policy.	– 2003: CAP Midterm Review: decoupling of income support, mandatory cross-compliance – 2004: Accession of 8 new Member States from Central Europe, plus Cyprus and Malta – 2007: Accession of Bulgaria and Romania – 2008: Health Check; Single Market Organisation comes into force – 2009: Lisbon Treaty

Source: adapted from Meester (2010), p.35, Silvis and Lapperre (2010), p.173, Thomson et al. (2010), pp.377-392

2.2.2 Implementation of the Last Reform Steps in the Member States

In the 2003 CAP reform a new system of support, the Single Payment Scheme (SPS) was introduced. As mentioned above, this system replaced most previously existing coupled aids. The SPS entered into force in 2005 and is currently implemented in 17 EU Member States. Most new Member States apply the Single Area Payment Scheme (SAPS) described below. In the SPS an annual payment is made to farmers based on the value of the payment entitlements held and activated by the farmer. In order to receive full payments under the SPS the cross-compliance obligations (Statutory Management Requirements and Good Agricultural and Environmental Conditions) have to be fulfilled by farmers.

When introducing the SPS the Member States could choose between three main models of calculating the payment entitlements (EC 2011 b):

- Historical model: based on the payments received by a farmer during a reference period resulting in different levels of support per hectare.
- Regional model: all payments received in a region divided by the number of eligible hectares resulting in a flat rate per hectare.
- Hybrid model: a mixture between the historical and the regional model. Hybrid models can be static or dynamic. Dynamic meaning that both elements are approximated towards a flat rate over time.

The Single Area Payment Scheme (SAPS) is a transitional, simplified income support scheme which was offered to new Member States joining the EU in 2004 and 2007. The levels of the single area payments in each country are obtained by dividing the country's annual financial envelope by its respective utilised agricultural area (EC 2011 c). On average, the level of EU direct payments per hectare is lower in the new than in the old Member States (EC 2011 d). This is partly the consequence of the historical reference from the period of price support and partly the consequence of political compromises during the EU enlargement process (Hofreither 2011). Member States using the SAPS have the possibility to top up direct payments (with the authorisation of the Commission) with complementary national direct payments. Most new Member States support livestock production or sectors in which the application of the standard EU support scheme would result in much higher support rates per hectare than the SAPS per area payment with complementary national direct payments.

The map in figure 1 shows which direct payment scheme is implemented in which EU Member State.

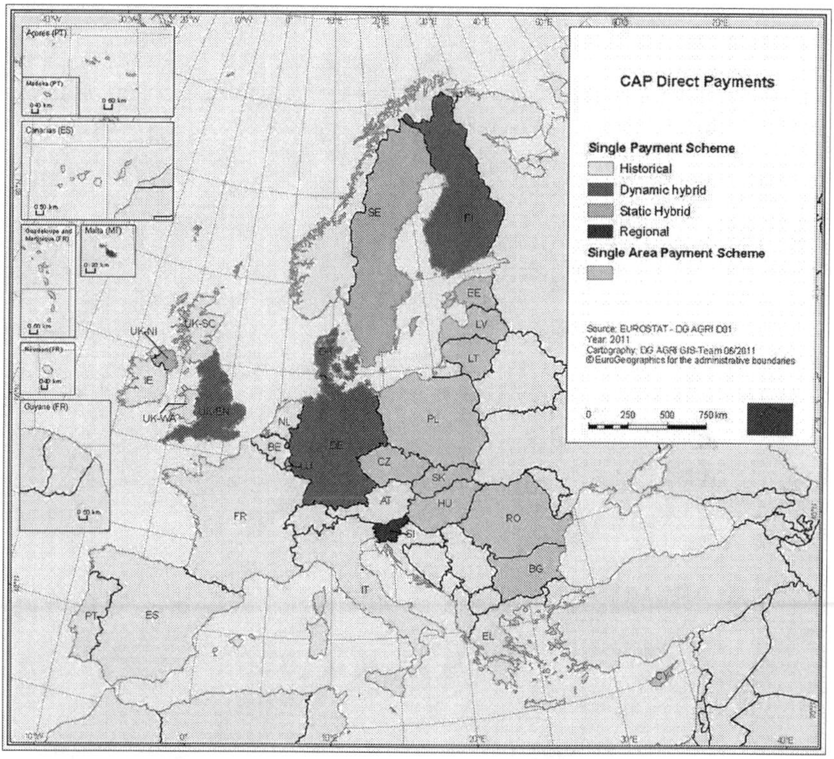

Figure 1: Implementation of Direct Payment Schemes in the EU Member States

Source: European Commission, Directorate General for Agriculture and Rural Development: http://ec.europa.eu/agriculture/direct-support/images/map-direct-payments_en.gif (accessed 28.11.2011)

The SPS allowed the Member States not only to choose between different models of calculating the payment entitlements but also allowed exceptions from full decoupling.

In the 2009 Health Check of the CAP further decoupling of all payments (except suckler cows, sheep and goat and cotton premia) as from 2012 was pursued. Through article 68 of Council Regulation No. 73/2009 the possibility for Member States to grant specific support using up to 10% of their national SPS budget was introduced. Resources that can be used for coupled support are limited to 3.5% of the national ceilings. Specific support can be granted for the following range of purposes (EC 2011 e):

- protecting or enhancing the environment,
- improving the quality of agricultural products,
- improving the marketing of agricultural products,
- practicing enhanced animal welfare standards,
- specific agricultural activities entailing additional agri-environmental benefits,
- payments for disadvantages affecting farmers in specific sectors (dairy, beef and veal, sheep and goat, rice) in economically or environmentally sensitive areas as well as for economically vulnerable types of farming,
- top-ups to existing SPS payment entitlements in areas where land abandonment is a threat,
- support for risk assurance in the form of contributions to crop, animal and plant insurance premia, support by way of mutual funds for animal and plant diseases and environmental incidents.

Table 1 in the annex provides an overview over the direct payment schemes, remaining coupled payments and the provision of specific support under articles 68-72 of Regulation (EC) No. 73/2009 in those ten Member States which were analysed in this study.

3 Synthesis of the Public Debate

This chapter contains the synthesis of the public debate in the ten Member States that were included in this analysis. The first section presents the results of a survey of EU citizens on the CAP reform, complementing the summary of the country reports, which is presented in the following sections.

3.1 Results of a Survey of EU Citizens (Eurobarometer)

In May 2011 almost 27,000 citizens in all 27 Member States were interviewed about their opinions on selected aspects of the reform package. These aspects were (EC 2011 g):

- The proposed capping of direct payments received per farm,
- A stronger link between direct payments and environmental protection (greening),
- The simplification of support mechanisms for small farms,
- The support of local food markets and products from mountain areas and additionally
- The transparency concerning the beneficiaries of CAP payments.

Although only very few aspects of the proposed reform were included in the survey and despite the fact that the questions were of a very general nature, the authors consider it valuable to present some of the key findings as they reflect, at least to some degree, the opinions held by the general public rather than those of experts and interest groups, which were mainly analysed in this project. This is especially relevant in the light of the fact that consumers who traditionally received little attention and consequently had very little impact on the agricultural policy-making process of the CAP have recently gained more weight. This can be shown with regard to food safety and product quality policies: Since public awareness of food safety problems grew in the 1990 s there has been increasing "pressure to create legislation and public standards for improved consumer safety and product quality, and to ensure that producer subsidies are consistent with this objective as an element of continuing CAP support" (Swinnen et al. 2010, p.264). Overall, the need to justify the continuing support of a small economic sector and to bring this support in line with society's expectations seems to be growing.

Some of the key findings of the survey are summarised in the box below.

Box: Key Findings of the Eurobarometer Survey on the CAP, May 2011[4]

- Almost half of the interviewed people (47%) support an upper limit of direct payments, though over a quarter (28%) opposes such a limit. There is very little distinction between respondents from new and old Member States with regard to that question.
- Slightly more people (44%) support a link between direct payments and environmental protection all across the EU as opposed to environmental protection that relates to specific areas only and is decided upon case by case (preferred by 33%). Also with regard to that question there is no real variation between old and new Member States. However, at individual country level, in five countries (Germany, Latvia, Hungary, Austria and Portugal) more people support the idea of subsidies being linked to environmental action only in specific regions, decided on a case-by-case basis.
- According to the respondents, additional assistance to small farms could be justified by the contributions of small farms to the social life in rural areas and to the rural economy as well as their need to modernise. Interestingly, respondents in the EU15 countries are more likely to argue that small farms play and important social and economic role than respondents from the new Member States.
- 55% of the respondents totally agree that the EU should encourage local markets and distribution channels, a further 37% say that they tend to agree. There is also wide agreement that labels identifying local products would be useful.
- 65% of the respondents think that buying products from mountain areas is beneficial, but many find them difficult to identify.
- A majority of respondents (62%) think that the names of beneficiaries and the amounts they receive should be publicly available.
-

Source: EC (2011 g)

3.2 Brief Characterisation of the Issues and Stakeholders Dominating the Debate in the Member States

In the following section the main characteristics of the public debate in the selected Member States are described based on the experts' national reports. This is done in order to provide an overview over the issues and stakeholders dominating the debate in the respective countries.

4 In some questions the respondents were given the opportunity to choose from a list of given answers with the option to spontaneously add an own answer or answer "don't know". In other questions the respondents were asked to indicate their level of agreement to a certain statement on a given scale.

Czech Republic

Stakeholders involved in the public debate in the Czech Republic are Czech members of the European Parliament, farmers' organisations, environmental NGOs, the Ministry of Agriculture and a research institute.

The two aspects most Czech stakeholders focus on are the question of a more equitable distribution of funds between old and new Member States and the proposed capping of direct payments, which most of the stakeholders strongly oppose. Other issues of concern characteristic for the Czech debate are the move from the current SAPS system to the system of payment entitlements for eligible hectares (as the development of black market structures is feared) and the demand for simplification and reduction of bureaucracy.

Finland

Apart from the Ministry of Agriculture and Forestry farmers' organisations are the most active stakeholders in the public debate on the future CAP in Finland. Environmental and animal welfare organisations are also active, but focus more on general aspects of agriculture rather than the CAP reform. Stakeholders involved in rural policy have so far participated surprisingly little in the public debate.

The wish to maintain agricultural production in the entire EU and income support for farmers is of major concern for some stakeholders, while others focus more on environmental aspects of the CAP. The greening proposals are contested. Two specific Finnish interests are the right to continue to pay national support for livestock producers in southern Finland and the right to pay LFA-support in the entire country. Also of importance for Finnish agriculture is the future of the sugar quota system. The questions of a ceiling on the direct payments received per farm and specific support for small farms do not receive much attention in the Finnish debate due to a farm structure with few very small and even fewer very large farms.

France

Apart from administrative and political bodies the public debate on the CAP in France is mostly influenced by farmers' unions, although environmental and development cooperation organisations have recently gained influence.

Owing to the relatively great social and economic importance of agriculture in France, French stakeholders have traditionally taken and still take the position that the CAP should remain strong both with regard to funding as well as market regulation instruments. While there is a broad consensus on some aspects, like the limitation of the provision of direct payments to "active farmers", there is disagreement with regard to the greening of direct payments, the question whether contributing to global food security through exports should be a priority for European agriculture and the move away from direct payments based on historical production towards area based payments. Rural development policies are of minor importance in the French public debate.

Germany

The main stakeholders contributing to the public debate in Germany are political and administrative bodies as well state agencies, farmers' associations, environmental and development cooperation NGOs as well as scientific councils and individual scientists.

One major issue in the debate is the demand for a harmonisation of the implementation of previous reform steps across Europe, mainly brought forward by farmers' organisations and political bodies, who also oppose a more equitable distribution of funds between old and new Member States. The greening proposals and the capping of direct payments are highly contested elements of the reform. With regard to second pillar policies the design of agri-environmental programmes and farm investment support schemes are issues of interest. A simplification of the CAP and a reduction of the bureaucratic burden are demanded by many stakeholders.

Greece

The public debate in Greece on the future CAP has been superseded by the discussions on the financial crisis.

Stakeholders contributing to the debate are the Ministry of Rural Development and Food, farmers' organisations, the media and representatives of political parties.

Issues dominating the debate are the distribution of funds between Member States and regions, especially the criteria used for the demarcation of regions in order to implement the regional direct payment model and the issue of eligibility of pastures for direct payments, which would result in a shift in resources and possibly conflicts. The definition of "active farmers" as well as the greening proposals are also highly contested. Possibly resulting from the current budget allocation and the doubts of some stakeholders concerning the authorities' abilities to design and implement adequate measures, rural development policy plays a minor part in the public debate in Greece.

Hungary

Stakeholders involved in the public debate on the CAP reform in Hungary are administrative and governmental bodies, experts and researchers (including the Agroeconomic Council), farmers' organisations as well as environmental and regional development NGOs.

Important issues with regard to agricultural policy in Hungary are the level of support granted to small farms, the distribution of power within the food chain, the support of local food production and markets, the support of the animal production sector as well as employment creation and reduction of poverty in rural areas. Concerning the current CAP reform many stakeholders demand equal treatment of old and new Member States, i.e. the same level of direct payments. Another overall dominating issue is the demand for a simplification of the CAP in order to reduce the bureaucratic burden.

Poland

Apart from the Ministry of Agriculture and Rural Development as the leading ministry on agricultural policy in the Polish government, farmers' unions and agricultural organisations, environmental, consumer, social and rural development non-governmental organisations as well as scientists participate in the public debate on the future CAP in Poland.

Major issues in the debate are the unequal distribution of direct payments between Member States and the still present connection of direct payments with historical production levels, support needed for small farms, the call for a reduction of bureaucracy (also discussed with regard to the greening proposals) as well as the importance of rural development policies and their relation to cohesion policies. There is generally strong support for a continuation of a Common Agricultural Policy (as opposed to a renationalisation of agricultural policy).

Slovenia

Apart from governmental and administrative bodies (mainly the Ministry of Agriculture, Forestry and Food, the Ministry of Environment and Spatial Planning and a state agency responsible for the implementation of agricultural policy measures) the Chamber of Agriculture and Forestry has an important role to play in the public debate on the future CAP in Slovenia. Other stakeholders active in the debate include the Rural Development Association of Slovenia, representing LEADER Local Action Groups, and scientists. Environmental organisations are less active in the current debate than they were in previous debates on agricultural policy.

Despite the fact that some voices within the government, e.g. the Ministry of Finance, have often called for a more fundamental CAP reform, Slovenia has mostly taken a rather conservative view on agricultural policy. This might partly be due to the fact that the Slovenian government seeks a consensus with agricultural interest groups in the opinion-forming process on agricultural policy.

The focus of the debate in Slovenia lies on the EC's proposals with regard to direct payments, especially the greening. Rural development issues were also discussed, but raised less controversy than policies with regard to direct payments. The proposals on market measures did not attract much attention in Slovenia, mainly because the significance of these measures for Slovenia is regarded as rather low compared to direct payments and rural development measures.

Spain

Apart from the Ministry of Agriculture the autonomous regions, that have far-reaching competences with regard to agricultural policy, are important stakeholders in the public debate in Spain, although the national position in the EU negotiations is only represented by the Spanish government. Other stakeholders active in the public debate are farmers' unions and a network of farming cooperatives. To a lesser extent also scientists, environmental organisations, rural development players and industry associations participate in the debate.

Most Spanish stakeholders take rather conservative positions towards the reform of the CAP and are mainly concerned with the redistributive effect changes in policy might have on the different Spanish regions and sectors. Important issues in the debate are the future of direct payments, especially the move from the historical model to a flat rate at national or regional level and market measures, especially ways to strengthen the position of producers in the food supply chain.

United Kingdom

One important characteristic of the UK public debate on the CAP reform are the diverging views and interests with regard to the CAP taken by the leading ministry in England and the devolved administrations of Scotland, Wales and Northern Ireland as well as the strong influence of the UK Treasury on the public opinion. The United Kingdom is represented in the EU Council of Ministers by the English Department for Environment, Food and Rural Affairs, but especially in the current round of the CAP reform, the English view, which is heavily dominated by the UK Treasury, has been criticised by the other devolved regions. The UK Treasury has traditionally taken the view that the CAP is an anachronism which should be abolished or at least be reduced in scope and scale of its funding. This position has dominated the public debate in the UK for so long that many commentators anticipate a long-term decline of the CAP, although this development is not at all inevitable from an EU perspective. Other important stakeholders are specialised environmental agencies of government, farming and landowning lobby groups, environmental NGOs and some groups representing local community interests.

Issues dominating the debate are the scale of support to agriculture, the function of and justification for direct payments, the best way to focus the CAP on the production of public goods and the role of the second pillar.

Table 2 provides an overview of the stakeholder groups that are predominantly active in the public debate on the future CAP in the Member States that were included in this analysis.

Table 2: Predominantly Active Stakeholders in the Public Debate in the Member States

Member State	Governmental and administrative bodies, political parties	Farmers' unions and related industry's organisations	Scientific advisory boards and individual scientists	Non-governmental organisations
Czech Republic	X	X	X	X
Finland	X	X		X With a more general focus on agriculture
France	X	X		X
Germany	X	X	X	X
Greece	X	X		
Hungary	X	X	X	X
Poland	X	X	X	X
Slovenia	X	X	X	X Rural development rather than environmental NGOs
Spain	X	X	X	X
United Kingdom	X	X		X

Source: Country Reports

3.3 Summary of Stakeholders' Positions

In the following sections the positions on different elements of the CAP reform held by various groups of stakeholders in the countries included in the study are summarised. The stakeholders are divided into the following groups:

- Governmental and administrative bodies as well as political parties
- Farmers' organisations and organisations of the agriculture and food related industry
- Scientific advisory boards and individual scientists
- Non-governmental organisations from the fields of environmental and nature protection, development cooperation and rural development

The summaries are based on the national reports, in which the various stakeholders included in the analysis are named and described as well as the position papers, press releases and other sources are listed (see Dwyer and Lewis 2011, Juvančič 2012, Lataste and Trouvé 2011, Liesivaara et al. 2011, Nurzyńska 2011, Ocsko 2011, Prazan 2011, Rutz et al. 2011, Viladomiu and Rosell 2011, Vlahos and Klonaris 2011).

3.3.1 Targets and Challenges of the CAP

In its Communication of November 2010 the Commission names the following challenges (EC 2010 a):

- **Food security**: contribution to the worldwide rising demand for food, provision of high quality and a wide choice of food products for EU citizens (including local products), competitiveness of the European agro food sector in times of an economic crisis and agricultural markets that are characterised by greater volatility and uncertainty.
- **Environment and climate change**: provision of public goods, negative environmental impacts of agriculture, mitigation of and adaptation to climate change.
- **Territorial balance**: agriculture as the driver of the rural economy and the basis of local traditions and identity in many areas of the EU.

The objectives set in the Communication are the following (ibid.):

- **Viable food production**: contribution to farm incomes, improving the competitiveness of the agricultural sector and enhancing its value share in the food supply chain, compensation of difficulties in areas suffering from specific natural constraints.
- **Sustainable management of natural resources and climate action**: provision of environmental public goods, green growth through innovation, climate change mitigation and adaptation.
- **Balanced territorial development**: support of rural employment, structural diversity in farming systems (improvement of the conditions for small farms and development of local markets).

In its legal proposals the Commission affirms the policy objectives named in the Communication and states that "the need to promote resource efficiency with a view to smart, sustainable and inclusive growth for EU agriculture and rural areas in line with the EU 2020 strategy" (EC 2011 h, p. 2) had emerged as a common theme throughout the inter-institutional debate and the stakeholder consultation that took place within the framework of the impact assessment. As shown in figure 2, taken from a slide show on the legal proposals published by the Directorate-General Agriculture and Rural Development of the European Commission, **en-**

hanced competitiveness, improved sustainability and greater effectiveness are set as the main objectives of the current reform in the legal proposals.

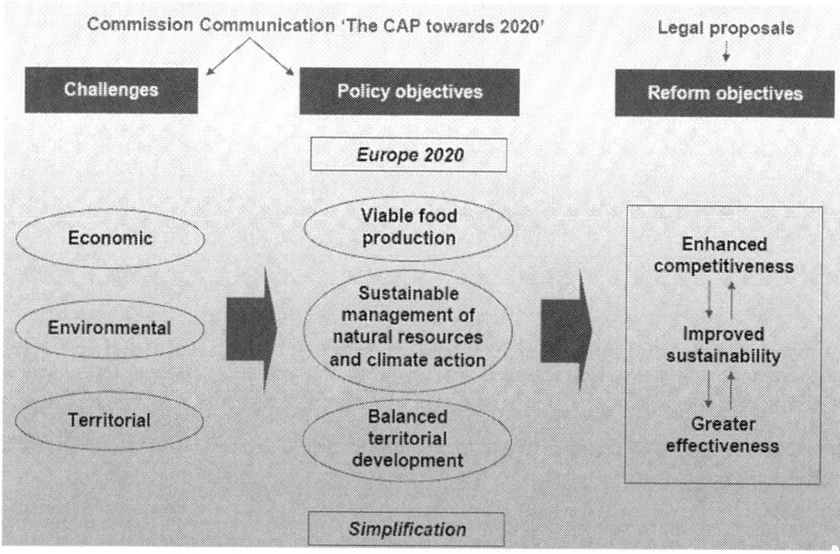

Figure 2: Challenges and Objectives of the CAP

Source: European Commission, Directorate-General Agriculture and Rural Development, http://ec.europa.eu/agriculture/cap-post-2013/legal-proposals/slide-show_en.pdf (accessed 12.10.2011), p.11

In a critical discourse analysis of speeches of two successive former Agriculture Commissioner's, Franz Fischler and Mariann Fischer Boel, Erjavec et al. (2009) find that the protectionist and productivist communication, which had dominated the CAP discourse for decades, was first replaced by the discourse of multifunctionality, but then moved towards a neoliberal orientation for the future CAP. When comparing these findings with some statements by the present Commissioner for agriculture, Dacian Cioloş, Rutz et al. (2012) detect a new focus of the Commissioner on issues of legitimacy, sustainability, transparency and equity (redistribution). The authors conclude that "the strength of the rhetoric in support of continuing aid for the farm sector" in some of the Commissioner's speeches "appears as a notable break from the previously dominant rhetoric of price cuts, progressive decoupling and shifting resources towards more targeted aid in the second pillar" (p.2).

The results of this study show that, overall, there is broad agreement with the challenges named and the objectives set by the Commission, but different aspects are stressed by some of the stakeholders.

Governmental and administrative bodies as well as political parties

The Ministry of Agriculture in the **Czech Republic** emphasises that increasing the competitiveness of the European agricultural sector and a more equal distribution of direct payments between Member States should be the most important objectives of the CAP reform. The Ministry also regards simplification of the policy and a reduction of the administrative burden to be important.

One aim of the CAP stressed by the Ministry of Agriculture in **Finland** is to maintain agricultural production in the entire EU. A reduction in the administrative burden is also considered an important objective of the reform.

The Ministry of Agriculture in **France** shares the challenges and targets identified by the Commission, but stresses the importance of decent incomes for farmers. In a statement that was removed from the homepage of the Ministry for the Environment as a consequence of strong criticism by farmers' organisations the Ministry calls for maintaining a financially strong CAP under the condition that it contributes to greater sustainability and focuses more on European consumption rather than on exports. The French parliament on the contrary stresses the importance to focus on the production capacity of European agriculture for both European and global food security, while regional governments, like the Mediterranean regions, would like to see their specific interest to be taken into account. An advisory board on agricultural policy made up of individuals representing different parts of society stresses the maintenance and possible increase of farm employment as a goal of the CAP and calls for support mechanisms for the cultivation of protein plants.

Governmental bodies in **Germany** largely share the challenges and targets identified by the EC, sometimes stressing the importance of increased competitiveness and productivity of the European agricultural sector. Simplification and a reduction in bureaucracy are also frequently named as objectives of the current reform. State agencies concerned with environmental and natural protection naturally emphasise the environmental challenges like climate change, soil and water protection and the preservation of biodiversity.

The challenges identified by the Commission are largely shared by most stakeholders in **Greece**. However, some left wing political parties actively involved in the public debate on the CAP in Greece consider competitiveness not to be a legitimate principle and argue that small family farms should be at the heart of the policy. According to the Ministry of Rural Development and Food the CAP should especially aim at keeping up agriculture in the entire EU and at promoting a balanced territorial development of rural areas through agriculture.

Governmental bodies in **Hungary** generally support the challenges and targets identified by the Commission, but highlight the importance of a simplification of the CAP and more efficient delivery. They argue that Hungary's interest lies in a strong Common Agricultural Policy. At the same time, they stress the importance of supporting certain national sectoral interests (such as wine production and planting rights, certain segments of the animal husbandry sector, fruit and vegetable and sugar production).The Parliamentary Commissioner for Future Generations (environmental ombudsman of the Hungarian parliament) takes a diverging and very critical position towards the CAP arguing that the current policies do not provide solutions to the challenges ahead or have even aggravated them, e.g. by funding agricultural practices that lead to an over-exploitation of natural resources. A reformed CAP should consequently implement the public money for public goods principle. With regard to the EU 2020 strategy the ombudsman points out that there is an insoluble conflict between sustainability and growth arguing that the priority of the CAP should lie on sustainability. Instead of 'feeding the world' through increased production, the EU should concentrate on its own food supply (here the ombudsman introduces a concept of "food-subsidiarity").

The Ministry of Agriculture and Rural Development in **Poland** calls for a more fundamental reform of the CAP in order to make it more growth oriented and to ensure that the EU agricultural sector becomes internationally competitive and to contribute to meeting the globally rising demand for food. It criticises that the Commission is more interested in ensuring transfers from the EU budget to the Member States than in reforming the CAP. In order to address the challenges ahead, like climate change, the Ministry sees the need to better coordinate the CAP with other EU policies in the fields of finance, trade and environmental protection. Like many stakeholders in Poland the Ministry demands a simplification of the CAP.

The government of **Slovenia** shares the challenges and targets identified by the Commission, but expresses concerns that the budget allocated to the CAP, especially in the field of rural development policy, might not be sufficient to achieve the set objectives.

The Ministry for the Environment and Rural and Marine Affairs as well as the regional governments in **Spain** largely share the challenges and targets identified by the Commission, but put special emphasis on ensuring sufficient farm incomes.

The official position of the government of the **United Kingdom** has long been to abolish the policy support of agriculture as a sector, replacing it by targeted public support for the provision of public goods. Similarly, an English government agency concerned with environmental protection stresses that a fundamental reform is needed moving the CAP from the principles of entitlement to payment to that of contractual payments for the provision of public goods. The Department for Environment, Food and Rural Affairs in England expresses disappointment that the Commission's proposals fall short of meeting the correctly identified challenges, namely to make farming more productive and protect the environment. This official

UK position, however, is no longer shared by the devolved administrations of Wales, Scotland and Northern Ireland.

Farmers' organisations and organisations of the agriculture and food related industry

Farmers' associations in the **Czech Republic** consider an increase in productivity and competitiveness to be the most important objectives of the CAP reform.

Like the Ministry of Agriculture, the farmers' organisations in **Finland** see the need to keep up agricultural production in the entire EU and to ensure adequate income support for farmers.

While farmers' unions in **France** generally agree with the objectives named by the Commission in its original Communication, there was considerable disappointment when the legal proposals were published, for example with regard to guaranteed funding of the CAP or with regard to a fairer distribution of direct payments between farms. The union representing the majority of farmers stresses that productivity should be maintained or increased to contribute to global food security, while a union representing small farms see the focus on sustainably ensuring food security within the EU. Organisations of the agriculture and food related industry stress the need for a competitive European agricultural sector with a high level of productivity fuelled by research and innovation.

The farmers' organisation representing the majority of farmers in **Germany** states that the current reform should primarily aim at the harmonisation of the implementation of previous reforms in the various Member States, especially regarding the implementation of decoupled area based single payments. Additionally, the organisation emphasises that the CAP should help farmers to be competitive in order to contribute to global food security and climate change through sustainable energy production.

Agricultural cooperatives in **Greece** criticise that the Commission's proposals do not contribute sufficiently to the creation of new wealth, the competitiveness of the European agricultural sector and food security, to employment and social sustainability in rural areas and to the reduction of inequalities within the EU.

Farmers' organisations in **Hungary** overall share the challenges and targets identified by the Commission. Some stress that a special focus of the CAP should lie on the support to young farmers or that the current CAP has failed in adequately supporting certain sectors of the animal husbandry sector, such as poultry and pig breeding. In a joined statement of the agricultural chambers of nine central European countries it is generally criticised that the currently proposed reform does not contribute sufficiently to the competitiveness of European farmers.

Farmers' associations in **Poland** stress the role European agriculture needs to play in ensuring global food security. The CAP should focus on ensuring food security, international competitiveness of European agriculture and equal conditions for all European farmers. The CAP must recognize that European farmers do not only produce food, but also a range of public goods.

Farmers' associations in **Slovenia** emphasise that all farms regardless of the type of production, sector or region shall have equal access to resources of both CAP pillars. A stronger emphasis should be put on stable agricultural prices, food security and farm incomes.

Farmers' unions in **Spain** consider the maintenance of viable farms to be the most important objective of the CAP, while an association representing agricultural cooperatives and a food industry's association put the emphasis on competitiveness. The contribution to global food security is also frequently mentioned by those stakeholders.

Some farmers' organisations in the **United Kingdom** broadly welcome the challenges and objectives identified by the Commission, but stress that agricultural productivity and competitiveness should be the main objectives of the CAP in the light of rising global demand for food. According to these organisations the Commission's proposals are not going to help to meet the objectives of smart, sustainable and inclusive growth. The Farmers' Union of Wales on the other hand stresses the importance of income support to farmers and the need to proactively support family farms by maintaining or increasing income support.

Scientific advisory boards and individual scientists

Scientists in **Finland** stress the need for a fundamental reform with direct payments being based on objective criteria.

Scientists from the think tank "Notre Europe"[5] in **France** demand a reduction in the CAP budget and a fundamental reform focusing on market failures as well as ethical and cohesion objectives. On the contrary an agriculture-oriented think tank sees stable farm incomes and increased production as main objectives of a financially strong CAP. The French Academy of Agriculture would like to see the CAP to be transformed into a common food policy targeting a broader range of issues, including the food programme for the most deprived persons and increased public demand for locally produced, high quality, nutritious food in mass catering. It insists on the necessity to regulate agricultural markets in order to achieve environmental and social objectives.

The scientific advisory board on agricultural policy in **Germany** largely agrees with the challenges and targets identified by the EC, but considers the policy proposals inappropriate to meet those challenges. The board calls for a fundamental reform moving away from income and distribution policy, which should according

5 Founded by Jaques Delors, "dedicated to European unity".

to the board be handled at national level, towards policies aiming at international competitiveness and the integration of the European agricultural sector into world markets. Scientific councils focusing on environmental issues demand a stronger focus on sustainability, e.g. by more ambitious measures for the preservation of biodiversity or by relating the CAP more closely to the EU Strategy for Sustainable Development.

Concerning the targets and challenges of the CAP scientists from **Hungary** emphasise a range of issues including food safety, competitiveness (institutional development, education), support for small farms, rural development (poverty reduction), environmental protection and the fight against climate change.

Some scientific voices from **Spain** call for a fundamental reform of the CAP moving away from ensuring stable farm incomes towards a policy of risk management. In the view of those stakeholders international competitiveness of the European agricultural sector should be the main aim of the CAP. Other important targets include territorial cohesion, rural diversification, quality, climate change and sustainable resource use, especially water.

Non-governmental organisations from the fields of environmental and nature protection, development cooperation and rural development

Not surprisingly, environmental organisations in **Finland** stress the importance to target agricultural support to environmental and climate change measures, while an organisation dealing with animal welfare issues wants to see animal welfare to play a more important role in the CAP.

Organisations promoting sustainable development, international solidarity as well as environmental and natural protection in **France** see the need for a fundamental reform in order to legitimise the CAP. The future CAP should focus on tackling environmental and climate challenges, generating employment, promoting rural development and food sovereignty both in Europe and in developing countries. An issue raised by some of the groups is the need to introduce support mechanisms for the cultivation of protein plants.

According to a platform of NGOs from the fields of farming (e.g. organic farming, small farms), environmental protection, animal welfare and development cooperation in **Germany** the CAP should not focus on international competitiveness, but be coherent in the sense that all policy measures of the first and second pillar have a positive impact on the environment and social justice, regionally, nationally and internationally. The NGOs stress that the CAP should also be coherent with the Millennium Development Goals and human rights, especially the right to food.

Environmental NGOs in **Hungary** would like to see the public money for public goods principle to be implemented more consequently and argue that the CAP should become part of a wider policy framework in order to address the complex problems in an integrated manner. Organisations of rural development stress that issues of rural development must not become subordinated to the agricultural sector.

NGOs concerned with social issues and environmental protection as well as organisations of organic farming in **Poland** call for a fundamental reform of the CAP promoting sustainable agriculture in all its dimensions. The CAP should consequently implement the public money for public goods and the polluter pays principles. One aspect emphasised by those stakeholders is the important role small family farms play in the preservation of biodiversity and the maintenance of social structures in rural areas.

Non-governmental organisations from the fields of environmental protection and rural development in **Slovenia** argue that greater emphasis should be put on sustainable management of natural resources in agriculture, including organic farming. An association representing Local Action Groups states that the future CAP should contribute to the following objectives: biodiversity instead of monocultures, provision of safe and tasty food, fair prices for agricultural producers worldwide, revival of villages and rural areas, nurturing of rural heritage and recognition of the economic and social role of small-scale farming. This stakeholder points out that the objectives of the CAP as laid down in the Commission's proposals are somewhat conflicting, e.g. greening versus intensification (competitiveness).

Environmental organisations from **Spain** stress the importance of the preservation of biodiversity as an objective of the CAP, whereas organisations promoting organic farming emphasise the need to support organic farming and to ensure the vitality of rural areas. A rural development forum considers multifunctionality of agriculture to be a priority of the CAP.

Environmental NGOs in the **United Kingdom** would like to see greater emphasis to be put on sustainable resource management, the preservation of biodiversity and cultural landscapes as well as on animal welfare. Also a stronger focus on climate change mitigation and adaptation measures is demanded. Generally, these stakeholders strongly criticise the Commission's proposals calling for a more fundamental reform as the current system of direct payments is seen as untargeted and inefficient.

3.3.2 Reform Orientation

The main points brought forward by the Commission in its 2010 Communication with regard to the overall architecture of the future CAP are (EC 2010 a):

- The continuation of the CAP in **two complementary pillars** with the first pillar containing the support annually paid to all farmers and the second pillar as the instrument to reach the community objectives and at the same time respond to the specific needs of the Member States on a multi-annual, programming and contractual basis.
- A **more equitable distribution** of funds between Member States, especially by ensuring that all Member States receive on average a minimum share of the EU average level of direct payments.

This general position was substantiated in the legal proposals in which the Commission proposes that the gap between the amount of direct payments received by some Member States and 90% of the EU average will be closed by one third, e.g. if a Member State currently receives an average amount per hectare that equals 75% of the EU average then this will gradually increase to 80% ('complete convergence' is scheduled for discussion for the time after 2020). These Member States will additionally be allowed to transfer up to 5% of their rural development envelope to their national envelope for direct payments. Obligatory modulation is replaced by the possibility for Member States to transfer up to 10% of their national envelope for pillar one to their rural development envelope (EC 2011 h and EC 2011 i).

With regard to the overall reform orientation the distribution of funds between Member States is the most controversially debated issue amongst the stakeholders included in this analysis. Only few suggestions regarding the general structure of the CAP are made.

Governmental and administrative bodies as well as political parties

The Ministry of Agriculture in the **Czech Republic** sharply criticises the unequal distribution of direct payments between old and new Member States and the extended transition period for adjustment. The Ministry supports the continuation of the two-pillar structure and does not want to introduce further co-financing from national budgets.

Governmental bodies in **Finland** stress the need for a more equitable distribution of direct payments between Member States. All Finnish stakeholders support the continuation of the structure of the CAP in two pillars and most support the current principles of co-financing.

The Ministry of Agriculture and the national parliament in **France** principally accept a more equal distribution of direct payments between Member States, but state that redistribution should take the situation of the agricultural sector in each Member State and the level of participation in the EU budget into account. The parliament opposes any increase in the co-financing share of Member States as this would lead to a renationalisation of the CAP and increase inequalities between regions and Member States. With regard to the structure of the CAP the Ministry for the Environment proposes to replace the current two-pillar structure by a single payment scheme made up of three components (basic income support, payments for environmental services and contractual payments for agro ecological transition). The national senate proposes a redefinition of the content of the two pillars with pillar one containing market measures and direct payments as well as the support for competitiveness currently contained in pillar two and pillar two comprising the current axis 2 and 3 measures.

The two-pillar structure of the CAP is hardly questioned by governmental bodies or other stakeholders in **Germany**. A more equitable distribution of EU funds between old and new Member States is opposed by most politicians in Germany, who argue that redistribution should only take place over a long period of time and only to a limited extent to avoid disruptions.

The Ministry of Rural Development and Food in **Greece** emphasises the need of a financially strong, EU-financed first pillar. While the Ministry recognizes that the shift from the historical to the regional model of direct payments will reduce inequalities, it considers a long enough transition period to be essential. Additionally the Ministry states that a link between public support for agriculture and the financial situation of a Member State should be established on the basis of solidarity and not as means of economic sanctions. In the view of a conservative political party an even distribution of funds between Member States is not necessarily a fair distribution. It is argued that the distribution process should take criteria like the contribution of the agricultural sector to the GDP of a Member State, the number and structural characteristics of farms, employment in agriculture or the share of farm land in environmentally sensitive areas, into account.

Governmental bodies in **Hungary** demand a more equal distribution of funds between Member States and stress that the overall support level for Hungary should not be reduced. The continuation of the CAP in two pillars is not questioned.

The Ministry of Agriculture and Rural Development in **Poland** strongly criticises the unequal distribution of EU funds between old and new Member States. The government considers it necessary to maintain the current structure of the CAP, i.e. all three elements of the current policy.

The government of **Slovenia** supports the continuation of the current two-pillar structure of the CAP. The government recognizes that the stated objective of a more equitable distribution of direct payments will lead to a reallocation of funds between Member States and states that a pragmatic approach of determining the national envelope will have to be found that takes the currently existing allocation into account. Overall, the prevailing opinion in Slovenia is not supportive towards a more equitable distribution of EU funds between old and new Member States.

Like most stakeholders in **Spain** the Ministry for the Environment Rural and Marine affairs is more concerned to ensure that the funds received by Spain and its regions are not diminished than with the question of a more equitable distribution of funds between Member States. In this respect the Ministry states that the distribution of funds should be based on objective, measurable criteria. Also like many Spanish stakeholders the Ministry supports the continuation of the CAP in two pillars.

In the view of the Department for Environment, Food and Rural Affairs in the **United Kingdom** and the UK Treasury direct payments under the first pillar of the CAP should be phased out over the next programming period. Pillar two should be enhanced and the principle of co-financing maintained. With regard to the distribution of funds between Member States the Department for Environment, Food and Rural Affairs supports a fair distribution under both pillars moving away from current historic allocations to objective criteria. In contrast to the official UK position arguing in favour of a drastic reduction of the overall CAP budget the devolved administrations stress that adequate funding is a prerequisite to meet the objectives of the CAP. They also see an ongoing justification for pillar one direct payments and thus argue in favour of continuing the two-pillar structure of the CAP. With regard to a redistribution of direct payments between Member States the Department for Agriculture and Rural Development in Northern Ireland argues that the current distribution reflects the intrinsic characteristics of agriculture in the various Member States and that balanced territorial development could not be achieved if there was a significant redistribution of funds between regions and territories.

Farmers' organisations and organisations of the agriculture and food related industry

Like the Ministry of Agriculture farmers' associations in the **Czech Republic** demand a fast implementation of an equal distribution of direct payments between new and old Member States and oppose any attempt to increase national co-financing of CAP measures.

While farmers' unions in **Finland** do not express an opinion on the distribution of direct payments between Member States, an association of the food industry states that the different production environments in the Member States should be taken into account.

The farmers' union representing the majority of farmers in **France** opposes a more equitable distribution of direct payments between Member States, whereas a union representing small farms supports a more equal distribution that should go hand in hand with a harmonisation of social, fiscal and environmental standards.

Farmers' organisations in **Germany** emphasise that the financial focus of the CAP should continue to lie on the first pillar. They oppose a more equal distribution of EU funds between old and new Member States as the distribution of funds should take differences in purchasing power and input costs across the Member States into account.

Farmers' associations in **Hungary** criticise the unequal support of new and old Member States. They do not question the current two-pillar system, but emphasise that pillar two funding should not be increased at the expense of pillar one.

Farmers' associations in **Poland** demand an equal level of direct payments for all farmers in the EU and a departure from historical criteria. They support the continuation of the CAP in two pillars and reject any attempts to renationalise the CAP.

Farmers' associations in **Spain** defend the current distribution of funds or simply state that Spain should continue to receive the same funds as currently. One argument frequently used to defend the level of funding is Spain's vulnerability towards climate change. Some organisations propose changes with regard to the content of the two pillars, e.g. by suggesting that agri-environmental measures should be part of pillar one or that regional development should not be part of the CAP, but of cohesion policies.

While some farmers' unions in the **United Kingdom** principally support greater equity in the distribution of direct payments between Member States others express concerns that the introduction of flat rate payments might not be sufficiently targeted to achieve policy objectives and suggest the introduction of targeted instruments that are considered as fair among Member States and farmers. Others claim that any attempt to harmonise the level of direct payments must recognise the differences between farming systems and associated production costs across the EU.

Scientific advisory boards and individual scientists

Like the governmental bodies some scientific voices in **Finland** call for a more equitable distribution of direct payments between the EU Member States.

As the only stakeholder in **France** the think tank "Notre Europe" promotes national co-financing as a general rule. With regard to the structure of the CAP the French Academy for Agriculture promotes a single policy instead of the current two-pillar system as it is argued that the market and non-market goods produced by agriculture are closely linked.

Scientists in **Hungary** propose possible alternatives to the current two-pillar structure, either arguing that a three-pillar structure (food markets, rural development, agri-environmental measures) would be more logical or suggesting to set up two additional pillars (one on risk management and one on social solidarity, essentially food vouchers for poor people).

Like many other stakeholders from **Poland** scientists see the need to base the allocation of EU funds within the CAP on fair and objective distribution criteria.

In opposition to most other stakeholders from **Spain** scientists from the University of Valencia suggest a reduction of the overall CAP budget, an increase in nationally co-financed measures or solely national measures. The future CAP should be implemented in three pillars with pillar three including transversal or comprehensive programmes.

Non-governmental organisations from the fields of environmental and nature protection, development cooperation and rural development

A group of environmental organisations in **France** proposes to replace the current two-pillar system of the CAP by a single payment scheme supporting environmental and social services provided by agriculture based on different levels of requirements.

In a report prepared for an organisation concerned with rural development in **Poland** a new (pyramid) -structure of support is suggested: a flat rate payment, payments for less-favoured areas, environmental payments as well as other targeted payments should all be financed under the first pillar of the CAP. With regard to a more equal distribution of funds between Member States this stakeholder suggests setting up an average basic direct payment per ha in the range of 80-120% of the EU average. Countries above 120% of the EU average could apply declining payments from their national budgets till 2017 when they would have to reach 120% of the EU average. Countries below the EU average could reallocate 10% of their rural development budget and apply supplementary payments financed from their national budgets and the EU budget (modified top-up payment).

Environmental NGOs in **Slovenia** suggest organising the CAP in one single pillar as the division in two pillars is seen as artificial and superfluous.

NGOs in **Spain** suggest a reform of the current two-pillar structure of the CAP. A forum on rural development wants to separate rural development policy from the CAP and become part of cohesion policies. The CAP should then be organised in one pillar, which would incorporate the current first pillar and the remaining parts of the second pillar (the current axis one and agri-environmental measures). This stakeholder also supports the redistribution of funds between old and new Member States. Organisations promoting organic farming also suggest a single pillar structure with five axes (basic farm and market support, innovation, information and investment, agri-environmental measures, farm diversification, LEADER approach). Environmental organisations propose one single pillar with the name of 'Common Rural Policy' which follows the principles of the current pillar two.

3.3.3 Direct Payments

The future design of direct payments receives the most attention in the Commission's 2010 Communication and consequently also in the following debate. The main proposals made by the Commission in the Communication are (EC 2010 a):

- The introduction of an upper ceiling of direct payments received per farm (**capping**) while taking the salaried labour intensity into account.
- Improved targeting of support to **"active farmers"**
- The introduction of a mandatory **greening** component of direct payments (annual non-contractual agri-environmental measures applicable in the entire EU)
- Additional income support for farmers in areas with **specific natural constraints**
- **Coupled support** for certain sectors that are considered particularly important in certain regions
- A simple and specific support scheme for **small farms**
- Simplification of **cross-compliance**

In its legal proposals of October 2012 (EC 2011 h and EC 2011 i) the Commission proposes that the current systems of SPS and SAPS will be replaced by a **basic payment scheme** operating on the basis of payment entitlements for eligible hectares after 2013. All Member States are supposed to move towards uniform payments per hectare at regional or national level by 2019.

The proposals mentioned above are substantiated as follows:

- Capping: the amount of support from the basic payment scheme received per farm is limited to 300 000 € per year. Payments higher than 150 000 € will be subject to progressive reductions. The costs of salaries in the previous year can be deducted before these reductions apply.
- "Active farmers": applicants whose CAP direct payments equal less than 5% of their total receipts from all non-agricultural income and who do not carry out at least the minimum activity will be excluded from the provision of direct payments.
- Greening:
  - Compulsory greening component of 30% of direct payments
  - The three measures proposed are:
    - Maintaining permanent grassland (with claim year 2014 as reference)
    - Crop diversification: at least three different crops, none of which must cover less than 5% of the arable land and the main one of which must not exceed 70% of the arable land
    - Maintaining 7% ecological focus areas of the eligible hectares of a farm, e.g. land left fallow, terraces, landscape features, buffer strips or afforested area.

  - Organic farmers will automatically receive the greening payments.
  - Farmers participating in the Small Farmers Scheme (see below) will be exempted from the greening obligations.
- Areas with specific natural constraints: Additional support for areas with natural constraints (as defined by rural development regulations) of up to 5% of national envelopes can be granted by Member States or regions.
- Coupled support: limited to 5% of the national envelope if the Member State currently provides 0-5% of coupled support, or up to 10% if the current level of coupled support is higher than 5%. The Commission may approve a higher rate if the Member States can show it is justified.
- Small farms: Any farmer claiming support in 2014 may decide to participate in the Small Farmers Scheme and will then receive an annual payment between 500 and 1000 €. The actual amount will be fixed by the Member States and can either be based on the average payment per beneficiary or on the national average payment per hectare for 3 ha. The total cost of the Small Farmers Scheme must not exceed 10% of the national envelope.
- Cross-compliance: The number of Statutory Management Rules will be reduced from 18 to 13 and the number of rules on Good Agricultural and Environmental Condition from 15 to 8. The Water Framework Directive and the Sustainable Use of Pesticides Directive are to be incorporated into cross-compliance rules once they have been fully applied in all Member States.
- **Young farmer scheme**: The Basic Payment to new entrant young farmers (under 40 years) should be topped up by an additional 25% for the first 5 years of installation. This is limited to a maximum of the average farm size in the respective Member State. This shall be funded by up to 2% of the national envelope.

The aspects that are discussed most controversially amongst the stakeholder included in this analysis are the proposed capping and greening of direct payments and the shift to fully decoupled uniform payments per hectare on a regional or national level.

Governmental and administrative bodies as well as political parties

The Ministry of Agriculture in the **Czech Republic** favours a direct payment model with flat rate payments based on regional and sectoral criteria. The national envelopes should be allocated based on the area of farmed agricultural land. Such a system is seen as simple, efficient and justifiable to EU citizens and third countries. The Ministry fiercely opposes the capping of direct payments as such a policy would interfere with farmers' ability to decide freely on the size of their farm or even might result in the artificial splitting up of agricultural holdings. Furthermore, such a policy would impair competitiveness and increase bureaucracy. The Ministry also expresses concerns whether the introduction of a definition for "active farmers" would actually be beneficial or simply increase bureaucracy. The greening of direct payments is principally welcomed by the Ministry of Agriculture. However, there is some criticism with regard to the design of the proposed obligations, especially the introduction of mandatory ecological focus areas which is seen as impeding competitiveness and increasing bureaucracy. The Ministry opposes additional payments to less-favoured areas in pillar one.

The Ministry of Agriculture in **Finland** would like to be able to provide coupled support to some nationally important sectors, like beef production. While both the Finnish government and the Ministry of Agriculture principally agree that there should be a ceiling on the direct payments received per farm, the Ministry calls for more research on that issue in order to assess the impacts such a ceiling would have on Finnish farms. Overall, this issue is not of great importance in Finland as Finnish farms are rather small compared to middle Europe (only 6% of all farms in Finland are larger than 100 hectares). With regard to the proposed greening of direct payments the Ministry of Agriculture was principally supportive, but changed its position after the concrete measures proposed were made public, because it fears that the greening will lead to an increase in bureaucracy and that the crop diversification obligation will be difficult to fulfil for highly specialised livestock farms in Finland. Additional direct payments to farmers suffering from specific natural constraints within pillar one are strongly opposed by the Finnish government and Ministry of Agriculture. Currently, LFA support is paid in the entire country as a co-financed measure within pillar two and a shift to pillar one and complete financing by the EU is feared to result in an overall reduction of support for Finnish farmers.

Governmental bodies in **France** want to maintain some coupled support for certain sectors. While some want to implement nationally or regionally uniform payments as quickly as possible, others demand greater flexibility. Like most French stakeholders governmental bodies support the limitation of the provision of direct payments to "active farmers", additional support for small farms and farms operating in areas with specific natural constraints within the first pillar. Interestingly, the Ministry of Agriculture does not position itself with regard to the capping of direct payments, while other governmental bodies and political parties wish to completely base the provision of direct payments on employment or at least take employment into account. The Ministry of Agriculture principally supports a greening of direct payments that is simple and takes the economic situation of farms' into account, but rejects the Commissions concrete proposals. On the contrary, the Ministry for the Environment calls for much stricter greening obligations.

The Federal Government of **Germany** and the governments of those federal states with an agricultural structure dominated by large farms reject the capping of direct payments arguing that direct payments serve as a remuneration for the production of public goods and that those public goods are produced on small farms and large farms alike. The idea of a link with employment is also dismissed by the government as this would impair competitiveness and increase bureaucracy. Other stakeholders from the fields of politics, depending on the political parties and/or regions they represent, take a more positive point of view on the capping and a link with employment. This also holds true for the position on the proposed greening: while the Federal Government reluctantly joined the discussion on the greening of direct payments as it believes that environmental goals can be achieved more effectively through the second pillar, other stakeholders, e.g. from the German green party, welcome the greening of direct payments. The proposal to limit the support to "active farmers" is questioned by many politicians for fear that this might negatively affect part-time farmers.

The Ministry of Agriculture and Food in **Greece** is sceptical towards the proposed definition of "active farmer" as a definition limiting support to the producers of food, fibre or energy might exclude those who manage land and allow biodiversity to thrive, but do not necessarily produce food, fibre or energy. The ministry suggests that both the definition of "active farmer" and small farms should be left to the Member States. The ministry proposes a lower limit for the capping of direct payments. The proposed greening of direct payments is considered as an additional financial and administrative burden on farmers. While the attitude of Greek stakeholders towards additional support for areas with specific natural constraints, young farmers and small farms is generally positive, the representatives of left wing parties consider the proposed measures to be ineffective.

The government in **Hungary** supports the introduction of an upper limit of direct payments per farm if the remaining funds can be used in line with national priorities. The limiting of support to "active farmers" is seen as a danger to part-time farmers. The proposals to especially support small farms and young farmers are principally welcomed. The possibility to continue to provide coupled support to certain sensitive sectors is also welcomed by Hungarian government representatives. Government officials generally accept the greening principle, but fear that the proposed obligations might impose additional costs and a growing administrative burden on farmers.

The Ministry of Agriculture and Rural Development in **Poland** criticises the Commission's proposals with regard to direct payments as the introduction of new elements like the greening obligations, the definition of "active farmers" or additional support for young farmers will make the policy design more complicated and increase bureaucracy. However, the Ministry principally welcomes the capping of direct payments for large farms and additional support for small farms.

The government of **Slovenia** holds the opinion that Member States should be granted flexibility with regard to more uniform direct payments, e.g. by allowing for a longer transition period or an only partial unification of the direct payments level with differentiation according to land use (permanent grass land or arable land). The government welcomes the proposals of the Commission with regard to additional support to young farmers, a special scheme for small farms and additional payments for areas suffering from specific natural constraints. The agency responsible for implementing the CAP, however, fears that the introduction of additional schemes of direct payments will increase the operational costs of implementing the CAP. The proposed definition of "active farmers" is dismissed by the Slovenian government as it does not contribute to a better targeting of those agricultural holdings that actually produce agricultural goods and non-commodity outputs linked to agricultural production. Additionally, the proposed definition would be difficult to implement. The government considers the proposed greening of direct payments acceptable in principle, but considers it important that Member States are given sufficient flexibility to take into account their specific natural and structural conditions. The Ministry of Environment and Spatial Planning points out that the mandatory crop rotation might cause additional pressure on Natura 2000 sites and areas designated under the Water Framework Directive due to the high demand for maize.

Governmental bodies in **Spain** do not take a uniform position with regard to the proposed capping of direct payments: While some do not express an opinion on that matter, one regional government opposes it as impeding competitiveness and another one supports it arguing that large farms produce less public goods per hectare than small farms. Generally, governmental bodies in Spain support the idea to limit the provision of direct payments to "active farmers", but propose different concepts. The national ministry refers to 'active agriculture'; one region speaks of 'professional farmers' and another region proposes an extra payment to 'farmers with agriculture as their main activity'. The definition proposed by the Commission is criticised as insufficient by all stakeholders. The greening proposals are dismissed by governmental bodies in Spain, because they will increase costs, reduce production and impede competitiveness. The Ministry for the Environment, Rural and Marine Affairs additionally argues that Spanish farmers are already doing enough for the environment, making additional obligations unnecessary. Additional direct payments for special environmental services or for areas suffering from specific natural constraints within pillar one are questioned, because the introduction of such payments might make the distinction between the two pillars unclear or create duplications. The central issue discussed with regard to the future of direct payments in Spain is the way to implement regionally homogenous direct payments. Both the national ministry and the regional governments have firmly rejected flat rate payments at national or regional level. Most stakeholders are looking for a way to couple or semi-couple direct payments as they regard decoupled direct payments to lack legitimacy and efficiency.

In the view of the Department for Environment, Food and Rural Affairs in the **United Kingdom** and the UK Treasury direct payments under the first pillar of the CAP should be phased out over the next programming period. The two ministries oppose the proposed capping of direct payments as this would have a negative effect upon efficiency. If the Commission wants to target direct payments only to "active farmers" Member States should be allowed to define the term in their particular contexts. Additional support to small farms is rejected on the grounds that the needs of small farms are best met through policies to improve their competitiveness. The greening proposals are also rejected as the environmental benefits are questioned. As mentioned earlier the devolved administrations of Wales, Scotland and Northern Ireland want to maintain direct income support, but recognise in a joint statement that the historic basis should be phased out. With regard to the capping of direct payments the minister within the Welsh assembly government expresses support in principle, but rejects an employment related adjustment as this would be impossible to implement in Wales where contract and self-employed labour prevail. The minister supports the idea that payments should be limited to people with farmed land as the principle source of economic livelihood. The Scottish government expresses concerns that the proposed capping as well as the proposed definition of "active farmer" will be difficult to implement and might be harmful for small farms. Both the Welsh and the Scottish government also express concerns that the greening obligations might lead to an increase in bureaucracy or be difficult to implement for small farms. The government of Northern Ireland is in favour of a ceiling of direct payments received per farm as payments higher than 100,000 € are difficult to justify and thus undermine the credibility of the CAP. The government is sceptical whether a robust definition of "active farmer" can be formulated that does not discriminate against part-time farmers.

Farmers' organisations and organisations of the agriculture and food related industry

Farmers' organisations in the **Czech Republic** sharply criticise the proposed capping of direct payments as such a policy would unjustifiably discriminate against large farms and increase administrative costs. One farmers' association also criticises that a link with employment would lead to unfavourable conditions for the most progressive farmers who pursue competitiveness through high input efficiency. The concept of limiting support to "active farmers" is welcomed by most farming organisations. The proposal to introduce a mandatory percentage of ecological focus areas is strongly criticised by Czech farmers' organisations as being contradictory to the increased demand for food and renewable energy.

Like the Ministry of Agriculture the farmers' unions in **Finland** want to maintain coupled support for certain sectors. They oppose the greening of direct payments. It is argued that such a greening would unnecessarily increase bureaucracy and costs for farmers, decrease productivity and would lead to an overlap of pillar one and two. One farmers' union argues that such a policy should be voluntary for Member States. Like the governmental bodies, farmers' argue that a change in the support for farms suffering from specific natural constraints would have a negative impact on Finnish farms.

With regard to direct payments the different positions between the majority of farmers' organisations in **France** and the union representing small farmers become especially evident. While the former are only willing to accept the introduction of nationally or regionally uniform decoupled payments over an extended period of time, the latter call for a fast implementation. While the majority of farmers' organisations in France do not refer to the capping of direct payments in their statements, the union representing small farms demands a stricter implementation than currently suggested by the EC. The greening of direct payments is opposed by the majority of farmers' unions in France as such obligations would endanger productivity and competitiveness. On the other hand, the farmers union representing small farms sees the greening measures as too weak to really have a positive impact on farming practices.

Like the Federal Government farmers' unions in **Germany** strongly oppose the proposed capping of direct payments. They also strongly criticise the greening of direct payments, especially the introduction of ecological focus areas, as this is seen to reduce productivity and competitiveness of the European agricultural sector.

The farmers' confederation in **Greece** principally supports the idea to limit the provision of direct payments to "active farmers". Agricultural cooperatives suggest defining "active farmer" as somebody who obtains more than 35% of his or her income from selling agricultural produce. This association also supports a lower maximum limit of direct payments per farm. The greening obligations are seen as an additional burden on European farmers weakening their competitiveness. The association of agricultural cooperatives suggests introducing a lower greening component of 10%, which could be raised to 20% after farmers had time to adjust. Overall, farmers' organisations are willing to accept the shift from the historical to a regional model, but express concerns that the demarcation of the regions will lead to internal conflicts.

Most producers' organisations in **Hungary** oppose the introduction of a ceiling on direct payments received per farm. In a joined statement of the agricultural chambers of nine central European countries it is argued that such a ceiling would be contradictory to economy of scales considerations and discriminate against some European farmers. At the same time the National Federation of Agricultural Cooperators and Producers suggests to link direct payments also to employment levels (subsidy payments per capita). In opposition to that opinion an association representing young farmers in Hungary agrees with the idea of a capping of direct payments. Farmers' organisations further oppose the proposed greening of direct payments as this is seen to impair the international competitiveness of the European agricultural sector and as counterproductive in times of increasing food demand. In the joined statement of the agricultural chambers it is suggested to include the greening obligations in pillar two as optional measures. In this statement the agricultural chambers support the idea to limit the provision of direct payments to "active farmers" only, but suggest that the definition of the term should be simplified.

Farmers' associations in **Poland** argue that the greening obligations are unnecessary as the existing cross-compliance rules ensure a sufficient level of environmental protection. Such obligations would lead to increased administrative costs and impair the competitiveness of European agriculture.

Farmers' organisations from **Slovenia** are concerned about the introduction of uniform area payments and support solutions that offer enough flexibility to minimise the negative effects of redistribution of funds between regions, sectors and farms. They are in favour of additional support to young farmers and areas with specific natural handicaps, but express reservations towards the proposed definition of "active farmers" (several proposals of a definition were made in a public consultation) and the special support scheme for small farms, because the latter might impede necessary structural change. With regard to the proposed greening obligations farmers' organisations are worried that this might lead to an increased administrative burden and claim that some types of farms will have difficulties implementing some of the proposed obligations, e.g. they propose that the 7% of ecological focus areas should be achieved on a national level and not on the level of individual farms. These organisations prefer the implementation of environmental measures in pillar two.

Some farmers' unions in **Spain** support the proposed capping of direct payments, but an association representing young farmers argues that such a policy would harm viable farms and joint enterprises. The proposal to couple the provision of direct payments with employment is widely supported by farmers' unions. Apart from the young farmers' association farmers' organisations support the idea to limit direct payments to "active farmers", but are critical of the definition proposed by the EC. One definition proposed is that companies and individuals who receive less than 10% of their income from agriculture should be excluded. The greening proposals are rejected by Spanish farmers' organisations as impeding competitiveness. Some organisations even argue that cross-compliance is unnecessary and should be removed as direct payments should unconditionally compensate farmers for increased production costs due to EU regulations. Two farmers' organisations explicitly position themselves against the decoupling of direct payments. They argue for example that large landowners will benefit from land based direct payments at the expense of productive, employment-creating agriculture.

Farmers' associations in the **United Kingdom** mainly oppose a ceiling on direct payments as this is seen as discriminatory and hinder necessary structural change. The proposal to limit payments to "active farmers" only is highly contested amongst the unions. The greening obligations are mainly dismissed as increasing costs, narrowing options for farmers and having negative consequences on the competitiveness of European agriculture.

Scientific advisory boards and individual scientists

In opposition to the opinion prevailing amongst most stakeholders in the **Czech Republic** the Institute for Agricultural Economics argues that only a very small number of Czech farms will be negatively affected by a ceiling of direct payments per farm if employment is taken into account.

Scientific voices from **Finland** call for a fundamental reform of direct payments that cut the link to historical production levels and are provided on the basis of objective criteria taking economic criteria, natural conditions and public goods into account.

Different models of direct payments are suggested by scientists in **France**, ranging from contractual payments focused on the maintenance of cultural landscapes to counter-cyclical payments.

The advisory board on agricultural policy in **Germany** argues in favour of decoupling all direct payments, which should be phased out as they were introduced as a policy measure for a transition period compensating farmers for a change in policy. This legitimisation is no longer valid. Policies aiming at a more just distribution of direct payments, like the capping or the additional support for small farms, should be based on income criteria. The proposed greening of direct payments is dismissed by the advisory council on agricultural policy on the grounds that such measures could be more efficiently implemented in the second pillar. The advisory council on biodiversity first saw the greening of direct payments as a chance to implement measures to preserve biodiversity, but sharply criticises the proposed obligations as ineffective (e.g. obligation on crop rotation) or even counterproductive (reference date for the prohibition to plough up permanent grass land lying in the future).

In a study carried out by the Research Institute for Agricultural Economics in **Hungary** the authors suggest to support farmers in each Member State equally by 200 € per hectare (decoupled support), setting some basic environmental, animal health, etc. requirements as eligibility criteria (cross-compliance). At the same time, related administration should be simplified (support would be based on the size of land used in a given year). They further suggest that Member States should have the possibility to set aside a certain percentage of their national envelope for support of specific industries. Differences concerning Member State support should be gradually eliminated. The funds that become available this way should be re-grouped to 'new challenges' within pillar two.

Scientists from **Poland** express concerns that the proposed greening obligations will significantly complicate the implementation of the direct payments scheme as new and more rigorous control systems would have to be in place. The Commission's proposals with regard to support to small farms are regarded as insufficient.

Scientists from the University of Valencia in **Spain** call for the gradual abolishment of direct payments moving to a system of contractual payments. During the transition period a ceiling on the direct payments received per farm should be introduced. Payments under contract (territorial and environmental payments) should be open to all landowners.

Non-governmental organisations from the fields of environmental and nature protection, development cooperation and rural development

Environmental NGOs in the **Czech Republic** express disappointment with the greening obligations proposed by the Commission as the measures are regarded as insufficient and ignoring some pressing issues such as animal welfare and soil degradation. The NGOs make suggestions on the design of appropriate measures that should be compulsory all over the EU and for all farmers (no exceptions for small farms).

Environmental organisations in **Finland** would like to see organic farming especially supported through coupled payments, while an animal welfare organisation argues that producers who apply higher animal welfare standards should receive higher subsidies. This organisation also argues that a ceiling on the direct payments received per farm would prevent the establishment of very large farms which would have a positive impact on animal welfare as they consider animal welfare to be better ensured on small farms. This stakeholder also supports the proposal to limit the provision of direct payments to "active farmers", whereas the environmental organisations argue that not only farmers, but everybody contributing to environmental protection should be entitled to CAP payments. Environmental organisations also argue for stricter cross-compliance rules, which is in line with the EC's greening proposal.

NGO-platforms in **France** consider it important to link the provision of direct payments to employment and favour a stricter implementation of the capping. They also call for stricter greening obligations as the now proposed measures will not change the current agricultural practices in France as they are already covered by cross-compliance.

NGOs in **Germany** welcome the proposed capping of direct payments and the proposed link with employment as well as the greening of direct payments. When the proposed greening obligations were made public, the NGOs, like the scientific advisory board on biodiversity, criticised them as ineffective or even counterproductive.

Environmental NGOs in **Hungary** state that the proposed greening obligations are insufficient to achieve the stated environmental goals.

Environmental and social NGOs in **Poland** argue that direct payments should be limited to "active farmers" and compensate for the provision of public goods. The NGOs support the capping of direct payments and the introduction of obligatory greening requirements. In a report prepared for an organisation concerned with rural development a new (pyramid) -structure of direct payment support is suggested: a flat rate payment, payments for less-favoured areas, environmental payments as well as other targeted payments should all be financed under the first pillar of the CAP. Farmers should have to submit an application for direct payments every seven years in order to reduce transaction costs. Additionally the introduction for a special support instrument for small farms is demanded.

Environmental NGOs in **Slovenia** call for amendments with regard to the proposed greening obligations as they are seen as insufficient, e.g. by applying the obligation on ecological focus areas also to intensively used grassland areas or by applying the greening obligations also to small and organic farms.

A rural development forum in **Spain** supports the capping of direct payments, the limitation of support to "active farmers" and the shift to the regional model. This stakeholder also strongly supports the greening obligations proposed by the Commission as they are seen to make agriculture more sustainable. Organisations promoting organic farming also support the capping of direct payments. They suggest moving to a system of single area payments, accompanied by an additional payment for organic farming, payments for rural areas of special public interest and other environmental payments. Environmental organisations also support the capping of direct payments, but argue that support should be granted to good stewards rather than be limited to "active farmers". They suggest implementing the regional model in a transition period aiming at the introduction of contractual payments based on the delivery of public goods and services.

Environmental NGOs in the **United Kingdom** argue that the current system of direct payments is unjustified and should be replaced by targeted payments aimed at the delivery of public goods and services. The proposals for greening pillar one are seen as weak and unlikely to deliver any tangible environmental benefits over and above cross-compliance.

3.3.4 Market Measures

In its 2010 Communication the Commission (EC 2010 a):

- States that the existing market measures should only be used as a **safety-net** in times of crisis and that there is a need to **streamline and simplify** the instruments currently in place
- Suggests the strengthening of **risk management tools** (as part of option 1)
- announces the publication of a revised **quality policy**
- affirms the previous decisions on the **elimination of the milk quota system** and on the **reform of the sugar market organisation**
- Stresses the need to **strengthen the position of agricultural producers** within the food supply chain.

In the legal proposals the following aspects are substantiated or added (EC 2011 i, EC 2011 j and AgE 2011 a):

- Certain sectoral aids are removed, e.g. skimmed milk, hops and silkworms.
- **Sugar quotas** are set to expire by 30th September 2015. After that white sugar will become eligible for private storage aid.
- The end of the milk quota system and the wine planting ban are affirmed.
- A new safeguard clause is introduced for all sectors to enable the Commission to take emergency measures to respond to general market disturbances. These measures will be funded from a **Crisis Reserve**.
- The product coverage for recognition of producer organisations and their associations as well as interbranch organisations by Member States is expanded to all sectors.
- Existing proposals on dairy (compulsory written contracts and strengthened bargaining power in the food chain) and on quality marketing standards are affirmed.
- The **school fruit scheme** and the **school milk scheme** are to be extended.

While the proposals to strengthen the producers' position in the food supply chain are generally welcomed by most stakeholders included in this analysis, there is a wide range of opinions on the scope, scale and nature of market instruments.

Governmental and administrative bodies as well as political parties

The Ministry of Agriculture in the **Czech Republic** sees the need to develop risk and crisis management tools complementing the already existing safety-net measures.

The Ministry of Agriculture in **Finland**, like most Finnish stakeholders, considers the strengthening of producers within the food supply chain a positive initiative taken by the Commission and would like to see risk management tools to be part of the future CAP. None of the Finnish stakeholders argues that the decision to eliminate the milk quota system should be reversed, but the Ministry of Agriculture would like to continue the sugar quota system until 2020. The governmental bodies also hold the opinion that some level of intervention policies should be maintained as a safety-net for farmers.

Governmental bodies in **France**, like almost all French stakeholders, argue in favour of strong market intervention, like supply management tools. However, while the Ministry of Agriculture principally welcomes the proposed urgency measures and risk management tools for farmers, other stakeholders, like the national parliament, call for guaranteed prices, public and private storage for longer periods and the introduction of counter-cyclical subsidies like implemented in the United States. Like other French stakeholders the national parliament proposes stronger environmental, sanitary, social and animal health rules on imports, which should be defended in the WTO negotiations.

Like most stakeholders in **Germany**, the Federal Government supports measures to increase quality production, improve labelling and to strengthen the role of producers in the food supply chain. The safety-net instruments currently available are sufficient from the government's view. Export subsidies should be abolished on the condition of an agreement in the WTO negotiations.

The Ministry of Rural Development and Food in **Greece** wants to continue the current market measures and additionally introduce risk management tools.

The government of **Hungary** supports the continuation of the sugar quota system. With regard to the wine market organisation Hungary does not support the proposed suspension of the previously envisaged new plantings rights by 2015. At the same time, government officials favour the idea of providing sector-specific support to certain sensitive national industries (e.g. within the animal husbandry sector) from the national envelope. The improvement of value added and safe food supply and market conditions are among the main strategic areas identified in the National Rural Strategy Concept.

Governmental bodies in **Poland** state that market intervention mechanism should be retained as a safety-net in the case of sharp price decreases or volatile prices. Promotion activities (both in the EU and on international markets) should be strengthened. In the face of new risk factors, such as climate change, advanced risk management tools should be introduced.

The government of **Slovenia** supports the retention of the existing market measures in the form of safety-nets. The government supports the proposed elimination of the sugar quota system in 2015, expecting that this will result in an improved long-term supply of sugar in all Member States, including those which have ceased sugar production. The government wants to maintain the current system of planting rights for wine as this is seen to stabilise the market. The government supports the

Commission's proposals to strengthen the role of producers in the food supply chain by strengthening producer and interbranch organisations.

The Ministry for the Environment, Rural and Marine affairs in **Spain**, like most Spanish stakeholders, criticises the Commission's proposals with regard to market measures as insufficient to effectively deal with increased price volatility. Both the national as well as the regional governments seek to strengthen market intervention tools such as intervention or public and private storage. Most regional governments are opposed to the removal of the existing supply restriction systems. Great emphasis is put on the need to strengthen the role of producers in the food supply chain. The measures proposed include the support of producers' organisations oriented towards the concentration of supply, to develop interbranch organisations, the implementation of standardised contracts and codes of good practice between food supply chain players and to increase transparency along the food supply chain. Regional governments also strongly support the development of new risk management tools. The position of the EU in multilateral and bilateral trade negotiations is discussed by most Spanish stakeholders focusing on the demand that imports to the EU should meet the same environmental, social, quality and safety requirements that the EU imposes on European farmers.

The Department for Environment, Food and Rural Affairs in the **United Kingdom** suggests streamlining and simplifying the system of market measures (fewer measures, used less frequently) and wants to abolish export subsidies as well as the sugar quota system. The development of private risk management tools should be time-limited. On the contrary, the Department for Agriculture and Rural Development Northern Ireland wants to maintain the current system of market measures.

Farmers' organisations and organisations of the agriculture and food related industry

Farmers' organisations in the **Czech Republic** welcome the Commission's proposals to strengthen the role of producers in the food supply chain and to introduce additional risk management tools.

While the strengthening of producers' position in the food supply chain is very important from the perspective of farmers' unions in **Finland**, an association of the food industry argues that the strengthening of producers has to be achieved without harming the overall competitiveness of the food supply chain. Overall, farmers' unions support the introduction of risk management tools, but one organisation argues that such tools are better suited for producer groups rather than for individual farmers. Like the Ministry of Agriculture the food industry's association would like to maintain the sugar quota system until 2020. Both the farmers' unions and the food industry want to keep up a certain level of intervention policies as a safety-net for farmers. With regard to the positions taken by the EU within the WTO negotiations farmers' organisations in Finland are concerned that the regulations imposed on food production in the EU will impair the competitiveness of European agricultural products compared to imported products and call for more research on the impacts of WTO commitments on agricultural production. The continuation of export subsidies is supported by the organisation representing the food industry.

Like the governmental bodies the farmers' organisations in **France** argue in favour of strong market intervention, including supply management tools. Several stakeholders criticise the removal of the milk quota system, the sugar quota system and the system of planting rights for wine.

The farmers' union representing the majority of farmers in **Germany** principally welcomes the Commission's proposals with regard to market measures, but demands to maintain the current sugar and wine market organisations until 2020. An association representing farmers' cooperatives takes a more cautious view on the proposed measures with regard to risk management tools and the role of producers arguing in favour of leaving the implementation of policy measures in those areas optional for Member States. This organisation also would like to see export subsidies maintained as a necessary tool to help farmers to cope with fluctuating prices.

The farmers' union in **Greece** wants to maintain or strengthen market measures, including export subsidies (until trading partners eliminate their own export support mechanisms) and intervention buying with higher intervention prices and broader product coverage. The organisation also demands the introduction of risk management tools. An organisation of young farmers emphasises the importance of collective forms of organisation, short value added chains and alternative marketing channels as well as the provision of training and advice.

Farmers' associations in **Hungary** support the proposals of the Commission to strengthen the role of producers in the food supply chain. They also argue that the needs of the animal husbandry sector, especially poultry and pig breeding should be better addressed.

Farmers' organisations in **Poland** demand (more) instruments to protect the income of farmers facing increasing volatility of agricultural prices. They also call for more efforts to be undertaken in order to strengthen the role of producers in the food supply chain.

Farmers' unions in **Spain** put great emphasis on the importance of market measures. All unions firmly oppose the elimination of the existing quota systems and the wine planting ban. Like the national and regional governments famers' associations claim that market measures should be strengthened, suggest a variety of measures to strengthen the role of producers in the food supply chain and demand that imported food products should be subject to the same standards as European products. The development of risk management tools is also supported by Spanish farmers' unions, for example by supported income insurance systems.

Farmers' organisations in the **United Kingdom** are generally supportive of measures to strengthen the role of producers in the food supply chain, e.g. by regulating contractual terms in the food sector.

Scientific advisory boards and individual scientists

The only stakeholder in **France** arguing in favour of liberalising markets are the researchers of the think tank "Notre Europe", who would like to see intervention mechanisms to be reduced to safety-nets that are only activated by an independent agency in times of crisis. The scientists also state that private risk management tools should be supported temporarily.

The scientific advisory board on agricultural policy in **Germany** argues in favour of abolishing all remaining quota systems and promoting exports by other means rather than export subsidies. Its members see risk management primarily as a task of the entrepreneur and suggest that supportive measures should only temporarily complement private efforts.

In **Hungary**, similarly to other stakeholders, some scientists emphasise the importance of providing sector-specific support to certain national industries. For instance, in its suggestion for a new priority framework, the Research Institute of Agricultural Economics suggests the allocation of a certain percentage of area based direct support to specific industries, similarly to the provision of Article 68 of the Council Regulation No 73/2009.

Scientists from the University of Valencia in **Spain** are the only Spanish stakeholders arguing in favour of increased market liberalisation, e.g. by eliminating the milk and sugar quota systems and the wine planting ban. Measures to improve product quality are seen by these stakeholders as a way to ensure competitiveness.

Non-governmental organisations from the fields of environmental and nature protection, development cooperation and rural development

While some stakeholders would like to see export subsidies reinforced, NGOs (alongside the farmers' union representing small farms) in **France** argue in favour of an end to export subsidies. Environmental NGOs would like to introduce a tax on imports that do not fulfil European environmental standards. While many stakeholders mention the need to strengthen producers' within the food supply chain, the NGOs and the farmers' union representing small farms claim that local food markets should be especially supported.

NGOs in **Germany** fear that subsidised risk management tools might constitute an incentive for farmers not to adopt precautionary measures and to favour high yielding cultivation systems based on high inputs. NGOs also criticise the planned abolishment of the sugar quota system as this is seen as only serving the interests of the European processing industry by keeping their input costs low. Especially those NGOs concerned with development cooperation demand the abolishment of all export subsidies. Some stakeholders even call for the introduction of export bans or export taxes on products benefiting from high direct payments.

NGOs in **Poland** want to strengthen the connection between producers and consumers by rebuilding local food chains.

NGOs in **Spain** suggest strengthening the role of producers' by supporting short food supply chains and local food systems. Organisations promoting organic farming seek to establish a coherent and easily to understand labelling and traceability system as a key element of the future policy. These organisations want to ban imports of agricultural products that contribute to the unsustainable use of natural resources and the destruction of small family farms and food security in developing countries. The only Spanish stakeholder explicitly stating that export subsidies should be abolished due to their negative impacts on farmers in developing countries is an environmental organisation.

3.3.5 Rural Development

The Commission's 2010 Communication contains only very few concrete proposals with regard to rural development policy. Some aspects mentioned are (EC 2010 a):

- A shift to a more outcome oriented approach by setting **quantified targets** at EU and programme level
- Basing the distribution of rural development funds on **objective criteria**
- Increased coherence between rural development policy and other EU policy (**common strategic framework**), while reducing bureaucracy
- The introduction of a risk **management** toolkit (income stabilisation, support of insurance instruments and mutual funds)
- Strengthening and simplifying **quality and promotion policies**

The legal proposals envisage the reorganisation of rural development policy as follows (EC 2011 i, EC 2011 k and AgE 2011 b):

- Integration of the EAFRD into the Common Strategic Framework also applicable for the European Regional Development Fund (ERDF), the European Social Fund (ESF), the Cohesion Fund (CF) and the European Maritime and Fisheries Fund (EMFF). In a **partnership contract** the Member States will outline the intended use of funds in the pursuit of the EU 2020 objectives.
- 5% of the EAFRD funds will be held back in a **performance reserve** until it can be proven that progress towards earlier agreed targets has been made.

- The former three axes with the minimum spending requirements on each axis are replaced by the **six priorities** listed below. These priorities and the quantified targets set against them are to be the basis of programming and ensure the link to the objectives of the Europe 2020 strategy. Member States or regions choose combinations of measures from a menu to design the rural development programmes. Priorities:
  - fostering knowledge transfer and innovation in agriculture, forestry and rural areas
  - enhancing competitiveness of all types of agriculture and enhancing farm viability
  - promoting food chain organisation and risk management in agriculture
  - restoring, preserving and enhancing ecosystems dependent on agriculture and forestry
  - promoting resource efficiency and supporting the shift towards a low-carbon and climate-resilient economy in the agriculture, food and forestry sectors
  - promoting social inclusion, poverty reduction and economic development in rural areas
- According to a press release by the European Commission explaining the main elements of the reform "Member States are still required to maintain 25% of their rural development envelope on issues related to land management and the fight against climate change" (EC 2011 i). However, it has been criticised by several stakeholders and also the European Court of Auditors that this recommendation to preserve the resources devoted to former axis two are only mentioned in the preamble of the draft regulation and not in the mandatory provisions (ECA 2012).
- At least 5% of the total EAFRD contribution to the rural development programme shall be reserved for LEADER.
- The EU **co-funding rates** will be 85% in less developed regions, the outermost regions and the smaller Aegean islands, and 50% in other regions for most payments, but can be higher for innovation and knowledge transfer, cooperation, establishing producer groups, young farmer installation grants and LEADER projects.
- Member States will have the possibility to design **sub-programmes** with higher support rates to address the needs of young farmers, small farmers, mountain areas and short supply chains
- Introduction of a new risk management toolkit including support to mutual funds and a new income stabilisation tool
- Introduction of **biophysical criteria** for the delimitation of areas facing natural constraints, including short length of the growing period, dryness and un-

favourable soil conditions. However, other areas affected by specific constraints can be eligible for support. These areas shall comprise farming areas which are homogeneous from the point of view of natural protection conditions and their total extent shall not exceed 10% of the area of the Member State concerned.

As the main changes proposed for rural development policy were only made public with the legal proposals in October 2011 only few concrete statements on rural development from relevant stakeholders were available of the time of writing of the country reports.

Governmental and administrative bodies as well as political parties

The Ministry of Agriculture in the **Czech Republic** supports a strong rural development policy as a tool for increasing the competitiveness of the agricultural sector and to deal with the challenges faced by rural areas, especially depopulation and unemployment. The Ministry demands to distribute funds for rural development based on objective criteria, particularly with regard to the need for modernisation of farms and rural areas. The proposed partner agreements between the EC and the Member States are eyed with suspicion as this is regarded as an additional step in the administrative process, thus making the system more complicated.

The governmental bodies in **Finland,** like many Finnish stakeholders, would like to link the provision of payments for agri-environmental programmes to biophysical criteria and to link LFA payments to climatic criteria. An issue of importance to the Finnish government is the inclusion of the objectives of the Baltic Sea Strategy in the CAP in order to reduce the negative impacts of agriculture (phosphorus and nitrogen spillage) on the Baltic Sea. The Ministry of Agriculture demands greater freedom of choice for the Member States with regard to appropriate policy measures within the second pillar and would like to see environmental subsidies directed to those areas where they have the highest impact. The Ministry of Agriculture also argues in favour of a better adaptation of regulations between EAFRD and the other EU funds.

Regional development policies do not attract much attention from governmental bodies in **France**. However, the advisory board and one of the regional governments would like to see more decision power with regard to the design and implementation of rural development programmes to be transferred to the regional level.

The linking of compensatory payments to biophysical and climatic criteria is questioned by the Federal Council of **Germany** as the initial situation differs too much between the regions and not only the comparison with other European regions but the difference to the neighbouring metropolitan areas matters. Like many German stakeholders, the Federal Government, sees the need to create stronger incentives for the participation in agri-environmental measures.

Governmental bodies in **Poland** stress the importance of rural development policies for the catching-up process of new Member States and for facing the new challenges. However, the Polish government sees the need to better coordinate rural development measures under the CAP with the EU's cohesion policy and to improve the targeting of second pillar measures. Representatives of local self-governance institutions would like to see the second pillar of the CAP to be strengthened and improve the targeting of rural development measures. Issues of importance are environmental protection and climate change, innovation and the improvement of infrastructure in rural areas as well as access of rural citizens to culture, education and services. The LEADER approach should be strengthened by increased funding for Local Action Groups and a simplification of administrative procedures. These stakeholders also advocate the creation of a multi-fund rural development policy in order to better address complex problems and to simplify the evaluation process.

The government of **Slovenia** supports the creation of a common strategic framework and agrees with the proposed priorities for rural development policies, including the possibility to set up schemes that address specific problems in Member States (young farmers, small farms, mountain areas, short/local supply chains).

National and regional governments in **Spain** see competitiveness of the agricultural sector as the main objective of the second pillar. The Ministry for the Environment, Rural and Marine affairs additionally considers the support of women and young people in the agricultural sector to be an important objective of rural development policies. The question whether compensatory payments should be linked to climatic and biophysical criteria does not attract much attention in the Spanish debate. Two regional governments, however, would like to include areas affected by socio-economic handicaps (risk of depopulation). Some governmental bodies favour the implementation of rural development policies in the form of 'territorial or global contracts', which are defined as a formal instrument which establishes the set of commitments between the government and the owner of a farm to guide and encourage their activity for sustainable rural development.

The Department for Environment, Food and Rural Affairs in the **United Kingdom** wants to strengthen rural development funding and policies specifically for the provision of public goods. The Ministry argues that Member States should be given the flexibility to allocate the funds in a way that best suits their requirements providing it is consistent with the objectives of the CAP. It would only support greater coordination between rural development policies and structural funds providing the controls of all funds were more risk based and proportionate, with a reduced administrative burden. An association representing local governments across the UK demands to increase the proportion of funds supporting rural economic and social development and diversification, to pursue a local approach driven by bottom-up priorities with a strengthened and broadened LEADER initiative, to simplify procedures and to better coordinate rural development programmes with other EU initiatives seeking to achieve similar outputs, such as structural funds.

Farmers' organisations and organisations of the agriculture and food related industry

Overall, farmers' organisations in **Finland** would like to maintain the current structure of the second pillar. One farmers' union argues similarly to the Ministry of Agriculture that Member States should have greater flexibility in choosing the appropriate policy instruments within the second pillar.

The farmers' union representing the majority of farmers in **Germany** argues that second pillar measures should focus more strongly on agriculture by fostering competitiveness and by reintroducing an incentive component for agri-environmental measures. The association opposes a redefinition of less-favoured areas on the basis of biophysical criteria.

Similarly, the farmers' union in **Greece** states that rural development should focus on agriculture.

Farmers' organisations in **Hungary** see that the rural development objectives of the CAP are important, but oppose a transfer of funds from pillar one to pillar two.

The agricultural chamber of **Poland** stresses the importance of rural development policies and argues in favour of great flexibility of Member States to design national or regional rural development programmes. Support for less-favoured areas should remain part of pillar two. A redefinition of those areas should be based on objective criteria. Other farmers' organisations emphasise the importance of the second pillar for the modernisation of the agro food sector.

Farmers' associations in **Slovenia** welcome the Commission's proposals on rural development policies and stress the importance of knowledge transfer to agriculture and forestry and advisory systems.

Like governmental bodies in **Spain** the Spanish farmers' unions consider competitiveness of the agricultural sector to be the top priority of rural development policy, some also naming the support of young farmers' start-ups as an objective. In the view of the Spanish farmers' organisations rural diversification measures should not be part of the CAP.

Scientific advisory boards and individual scientists

Scientific voices from **Finland** support the proposal to link the provision of compensatory payments to biophysical and climatic criteria and measures for rural areas to objective criteria and the achievement of concrete targets.

The think tank "Notre Europe" in **France** wants to promote bottom-up integrative projects for rural development.

In opposition to the farmers' unions the scientific advisory board on agricultural policy in **Germany** demands a truly multisectoral approach to rural development.

Scientific voices from **Hungary** stress the importance of integrated rural development approaches and argue that the relationship between rural development and cohesion policies needs to be clarified. Rather than offering a 'common menu of measures' integrated and well targeted programmes should be designed, taking local needs better into account. A particularly important goal of rural development policies should be the reduction of poverty.

Non-governmental organisations from the fields of environmental and nature protection, development cooperation and rural development

Environmental NGOs in the **Czech Republic** would like to increase the budget for pillar two measures aiming at the preservation of natural resources, improve the targeting of agri-environmental measures and suggest animal welfare as a new priority for the second pillar.

Like the Finnish government environmental and animal welfare organisations in **Finland** would like to see a link between compensatory payments and biophysical and climatic criteria as well as a link between measures for rural areas with objective criteria and the achievement of concrete targets to be established. Overall, environmental organisations demand that public support should be better targeted at the provision of ecosystem services.

Some environmental NGOs in **France** would like 50% of all second pillar funds to be spent on environmental protection.

NGOs in **Germany** propose a structural and financial strengthening of the second pillar with ambitious agri-environmental and animal welfare measures and a focus on integrated rural development approaches. Farm investment support should be limited to measures that have a positive environmental impact or create jobs. Systematic approaches, like organic farming, should be especially supported and the eligibility of assistance in the second pillar broadened, e.g. by funding a greater variety of measures like investments, management or monitoring.

Organisations of rural development in **Hungary** stress the importance of endogenous development of local communities and that not only the devolution of competences, but also the necessary resources are a prerequisite for the successful implementation of the subsidiarity principle. These organisations also criticise that the LEADER approach has received insufficient attention as a suitable tool for achieving the goals of the Europe 2020 strategy.

NGOs concerned with rural development in **Poland** advocate a new approach to development: At EU level strategic development goals should be determined reflecting the goals of competitiveness, sustainable development and cohesion and offer diversified sources of financing. Member States and regions should be responsible for creating strategic rural development frameworks to enable the flexible implementation of local strategies which should combine both urban and rural areas. The LEADER approach, which can not only be used to manage rural development funds but also for other public programmes, and the participation of civil society should be promoted.

Environmental organisations in **Slovenia** express some concerns over the proposed changes in rural development policies. For example, the priorities 'efficiency in water use' and 'efficiency of energy use in agriculture and food production' could be implemented in a way that focuses on competitiveness while bringing no wider environmental benefits or even causing harm (e.g. 'efficiency in water use' could be interpreted as 'more irrigation' and 'efficiency in energy use' could be interpreted as 'increasing the size of livestock housing blocks'). It is also criticised that no concrete proposals were made by the Commission on how to evaluate the progress towards environmental priorities. An organisation of rural development argues that the different policies affecting rural development should be better coordinated in an integrated approach towards rural development.

Environmental NGOs and organisations promoting organic farming in **Spain** consider sustainability and the delivery of public goods to be the most important aims of rural development. A forum on rural development argues that a holistic and integrated approach to rural development should be a key feature of the future rural development policy of the EU, which in their view should no longer be part of the CAP.

Environmental NGOs in the **United Kingdom** criticise the removal of the requirement to spend a minimum share of pillar two funding on axis two, the lack of explicit reference to targeting aid towards High Nature Value areas and the addition of measures for income stabilisation and risk management into pillar two which will, in their view, dilute its purpose.

3.4 Conclusions Drawn from the Synthesis of Country Reports

The range of opinions presented in this study is truly broad. At the one end of the spectrum the debate in countries like Spain or France is dominated by the call for strongly interventionists policies protecting European farmers from international competition and volatile prices, while at the other end most stakeholders in the United Kingdom try to find ways to efficiently target the public funds provided by the CAP on the provision of public goods and services. In many countries agricultural economists supporting the liberalisation of the EU agricultural markets and making European farms competitive through research and quality oriented policies, accompanied by measures to mitigate the effects of market failures, are alone with this opinion. While environmental and other NGOs frequently also demand a more fundamental reform and improved targeting of the CAP they often favour strict environmental and social regulations both in the EU and with regard to international agricultural trade over market liberalisation.

Fundamental differences also become evident with regard to whether increased productivity or multifunctionality should be the main objective of agriculture and therefore agricultural policy in the EU. While the former objective is stressed by most farmers' organisations and many governments, the latter is favoured by civil society organisations from the fields of environmental protection, development cooperation and rural development and sometimes scientists. This question is closely connected to the question whether European agriculture and thus the CAP should contribute to global food security by increased production. While this outlook is taken by the majority of farmers' organisations, other stakeholders promote concepts similar to the concept of food sovereignty, meaning the right of peoples to define their own food systems and agricultural policies in order to feed themselves by their own means.

Additionally, national characteristics strongly influence the positions taken by national stakeholders on proposals like the capping of direct payments or the implementation of regional flat rates. One factor influencing the positions taken on agricultural policy by the various stakeholders are, naturally, the prevailing climatic conditions and the resulting challenges, e.g. water scarcity in Spain or the generally unfavourable conditions for agricultural production in Finland. While the new Member States struggle with the consequences of political transition and the resulting agricultural structures and ownership patterns, e.g. the large farms/small farms- dichotomy in Hungary, others have to deal with specific characteristics of their administration systems, e.g. the lack of a properly implemented land register in Greece.

The position taken on the proposed greening of direct payments is not so much influenced by national characteristics, but more by sectoral interests. While farmers' unions object to such a proposal in principle and specifically the proposed measures, especially the introduction of mandatory ecological focus areas, environmental NGOs and specialised agencies originally welcomed the idea. In the end, however, almost nobody seemed to be content with the proposed greening obligations: while farmers' unions and governments criticise them as either unnecessary or as impeding productivity and competitiveness, environmental organisations dismiss them as ineffective or even counter-productive.

With respect to the proposal of the Commission to limit direct payments support to "active farmers", many stakeholders welcome the underlying principle, although some environmental NGOs and some scientists claim that everybody who provides the public goods and services demanded by society should be remunerated for doing so. Similarly to the debate on the greening of direct payments hardly anybody seems to be happy with the definition of "active farmer" proposed by the Commission, either because it is regarded as unduly discriminating against part-time farmers or because a more rigorous definition focusing the support on the professional producers of agricultural goods is demanded.

In the field of rural development policy, that overall attracts more attention in the new Member States where issues such as poverty and depopulation of rural areas are more pressing, the parting line runs between those stakeholders advocating a multisectoral, integrated approach to rural development with bottom-up implementation (like practiced in the LEADER programme) and those stakeholders that want to see agriculture and the improvement of its competitiveness at the heart of rural development.

The only issue that almost all stakeholders from all countries seem to agree on at first glance is the need for a substantial simplification of the CAP leading to a reduced administrative burden. However, very few specific suggestions are made on how such a simplification could be achieved. And if, they are often contradictory: while farmers' unions often call for a simplification, often meaning a reduction, of cross-compliance, environmental and rural development NGOs are more likely to call for stricter environmental rules and see possibilities for simplification in the implementation and monitoring of rural development programmes.

Even although only ten of the 27 Member States of the EU have been included in this analysis it becomes evident what a difficult task it is to decide upon a CAP reform that is not merely a political compromise resulting from a fight over the allocation of resources, but is based on a clear vision of what the objectives of a common European agricultural policy should be and what policy instruments could be employed to reach these objectives. However, while it still seems that, despite all the differences presented above, the positions taken by the national governments are dominated by the wish to ensure the highest possible reflow of money from the EU budget, while at the same time allowing for the greatest possible flexibility with regard to the implementation of CAP policies at the national level, there is some hope that international alliances, e.g. of farmers' unions or environmental NGOs, will give weight to other arguments. This hope is, in the authors' opinion, especially justified as the Lisbon Treaty has strengthened the power of the European Parliament in the decision making process on agricultural policy. It is now up to the members of that parliament to take all the arguments put forward by the various interest groups and the interests of the European taxpayers (!) and consumers, which often remain unspoken, into account. Doing so will, hopefully, positively influence the future course of the Common Agricultural Policy.

4 Closing Conference: Summary of Results

As mentioned above, the findings of the synthesis report formed the basis for an international conference on the CAP reform held in March 2012. This section summarises the main results of the conference.

In addition to commenting statements by representatives from different political levels on CAP reform and the synthesis report the Commission's proposals on the greening of direct payments, the capping and the limitation of support to "active farmers" as well as the proposals for the second pillar were discussed in more detail in working groups. The greening was generally seen more positive by the participants of the conference than by the stakeholder groups analysed in the country reports. In particular, the greening of the first pillar offers the chance to ensure that also areas with intensive agricultural production are reached and therefore to achieve a broad effect across the whole of the EU. Also a base line with a new higher environmental reference level to build on with the agri-environmental measures of pillar two could be established. Some suggestions for improvements, which might make the greening more effective and more acceptable for farmers, were made. One example was to allow local groups of farmers to organise themselves in order to fulfil the greening obligation of 7% ecological focus areas. This could, on the one hand, increase the effectiveness of ecological focus areas and the result could potentially be of much greater value if pursued on a landscape level and, on the other hand it would offer farmers more flexibility. Another suggestion was to allow certain forms of sustainable agricultural production on ecological focus areas, e.g. the cultivation of legumes.

With regard to the capping and "active farmers" proposals the participants recognised the Commission's intention to achieve a fairer distribution of direct payments between farmers', which might improve the social acceptance of the CAP. However, the proposed measures in their current form were criticised as poorly-targeted, overly bureaucratic or likely to have unintended negative effects, like the artificial splitting up of large agricultural holdings. It was therefore suggested to leave the definition of the term "active farmer" to the individual Member States. Alternatively, the Member States could be encouraged to make use of the already existing legal possibilities to exclude certain recipients from direct payments support. Overall, it became evident in the discussions on both the greening as well as the distribution of direct payments between farmers that stringent and consistent decisions on the future of direct payments can only be made if the function of direct payments is clearly defined.

The new design of the second pillar proposed by the Commission was seen to have positive potential, but the participants also argued that in order to make use of this potential "guard rails" and further clarifications are needed. A positive aspect mentioned was that greater flexibility allows adjusting the programmes to national/regional specificities. However, the new architecture also poses risks, e.g. in countries where efficient evaluation systems are not in place, or the danger of one-sided rural development programmes. Participants agreed that the introduction of greening obligations in the first pillar makes it necessary to reconsider the design of agri-environmental measures in pillar two. A chance could be that more demanding and target oriented measures could now be offered as voluntary agri-environmental measures in pillar two (IfLS et al. 2012).

5 Conclusions and Recommendations

The involvement of various stakeholder groups, from within and outside the agricultural sector, in this vivid and critical discussion on the current CAP reform shows how important the future development of the agricultural policy of the European Union is regarded to be and that the CAP faces great intrinsic and external challenges. Are financial transfers to a declining agricultural sector no longer justified? Or are the funds needed to remunerate farmers for the provision of valuable public goods? How should those funds be distributed between Member States and between farmers? How can the CAP contribute to meeting global challenges like food insecurity, increasing scarcity of resources and climate change? These are just a few of the very fundamental questions that are at the core of the debate on the future CAP.

In order to summarise the results of this research project the authors would like to highlight the following recommendations that were deducted from both the written assessment of the public debate in the ten selected Member States as well as the closing conference:

- **There is the need to develop a long term strategy or vision for the EU Common Agricultural Policy.** If such a strategy is not developed the outcome of any reform attempt is likely to be characterised by inconsistent compromises dominated by the specific interests of powerful Member States or lobby groups.
- **It is necessary to reconsider the function of direct payments.** Only if it is decided and clearly communicated what purpose direct payments should fulfil, consistent and justifiable decisions on the future of direct payments can be made. Are direct payments a compensation measure for a change in policy, as originally intended, a permanent income support measure or do they serve as remuneration for the provision of public goods? This concerns, inter alia, the question of who should be entitled to direct payments in the future, e.g. "active" farmers or "good stewards", and what distribution criteria, e.g. land size or employment numbers, are appropriate.
- Food security is not only about increasing production. **It is necessary to ensure that the CAP supports the realisation of human rights, especially the right to food in all its dimensions.** Self- determined access to high quality food and environmental sustainability as the basis for long term food security must not be neglected. In this context it is important to note that food security is not only relevant in a global context, but, in the opinion of many stakeholders, also in-

cludes the provision of EU citizens with nutritious, safe, tasty and sustainably produced food that helps to preserve cultural identity and traditional landscapes.

- On the one hand **a clear focus of the policy on EU objectives** is needed in order to avoid specific national interest from receiving too much attention. On the other hand the Common Agricultural Policy must leave **sufficient room for Member States to address their specific needs**, particularly in the case of the new Member States.
- **In order to reduce the complexity of the policy and the resulting administrative burden the CAP should move from an input- and measure- oriented policy to a target-oriented one.** Changes in policy should be assessed on the basis of their cost-effectiveness. Implementation should take place along the lines of the "management by objectives" approach. Evaluation should primarily focus on achievements.
- There is a strong demand for greater distributive justice which is seen to increase the social and political acceptance of the CAP. **However, the measures proposed by the European Commission, like the capping of direct payments received per farm and the limitation of support to "active farmers" are, at least in their current form, inappropriate.**
- The capping of direct payments is likely to have unintended consequences resulting from avoidance behaviour by affected farmers, e.g. the artificial splitting up of large holdings or pseudo-employment. Ways to minimise such behaviour would probably involve excessive administrative efforts.
- In order to exclude certain recipients from direct payment support Member States could be encouraged to make use of the already existing legal possibilities. The current direct payments regulation allows Member States, as laid down in article 28 (2), to establish "appropriate objective and non-discriminatory criteria" to exclude legal or natural persons with only minimal agricultural activity from direct payments support. Alternatively, the definition of the term "active farmer" could be left to Member States. The compilation of a negative list by the European Commission, as recently suggested, might be helpful to achieve the purpose of the "active farmer" definition with less administrative effort. However, it must be stated once again, that a stringent and consistent decision about who should be entitled to direct payment support can only be made if the objectives of direct payments are clearly defined.
- **The greening of direct payments, as a further stage after the decoupling of direct payments and the introduction of cross-compliance, offers the chance to systematically integrate environmental objectives into the first pillar of the CAP.** The greening has the potential of reaching areas with intensive agricultural production and therefore achieving a broad effect across the whole of Europe. If the potentially positive environmental benefits of the

greening obligations are not realised, as the measures are watered down in the political process, there is the risk that the public acceptance of direct payments to agriculture further diminishes.

- **Improvements that could make the greening obligations both better targeted as well as more acceptable to farmers should be considered**. Allowing for sustainable production on ecological focus areas could help to minimise the conflict of objectives between viable agricultural production and environmental protection. Allowing local groups of farmers to allocate the ecological focus areas between them could both increase the flexibility of farmers in implementing the measure as well as enhance its environmental benefits. If a greater choice of greening measures were offered at Member State or farmer level, as it is demanded by some stakeholders, it must be made sure that the environmental effects of the offered measures are equivalent.
- The greening of direct payments should establish a new, **higher baseline for the agri-environmental measures of pillar two**. In order to secure that more demanding agri-environmental measures remain attractive the introduction of an incentive component would be important.
- **The second pillar generally suffers from inconsistencies** as it currently contains an extremely broad range of policy measures, that sometimes pursue contradictory objectives (e.g. in the case of investment support and agri-environmental programmes). This problem should be tackled, for example by making sure that all investment support is in line with the environmental goals pursued by the policy.
- **Co-financing rates must reflect EU priorities** and ensure that all Member States and regions have an incentive to pursue those objectives that are regarded most important from an EU perspective. Possible consequences would be higher EU co-financing rates for those agri-environmental measures or innovative cooperative measures which contribute to the fulfilment of declared EU objectives, such as the challenges of climate change, sustainable production of renewable energy, water management and biodiversity.
- The new architecture of the second pillar with greater flexibility for the Member States and the multi-fund approach offers chances, but also poses risks. It will be necessary to carefully assess whether the hoped for results are realised or whether the new structure leads to one-sided rural development programmes or standard programmes that have merely been relabelled to fit the new priorities.

The authors hope that the changing nature of the CAP debate, that now involves more and a far broader range of stakeholders than in former times, and the new institutional setting that gives more decision making power to the European Parliament will lead to a CAP reform that sets the Common Agricultural Policy on the right path to meet the current and coming challenges as well as possible.

6 References

AgE (Agra-Europe) (2011 a): EU-Verordnungsentwurf über eine gemeinsame Marktorganisation. Agra-Europe 43/11, 24.10.2011, Dokumentation.

AgE (Agra-Europe) (2011 b): EU-Vorschläge zur ländlichen Entwicklung nach 2013. Agra-Europe 44/11, 31.10.2011. Dokumentation.

Dwyer, Janet; Lewis, Nick (2011): Synthesis and assessment of the public debate on the reform of the CAP after 2013: United Kingdom. Gloucester, http://www.ifls.de/downloads.html?&L=1, 33 pp.

EC (European Commission) (2010 a): Communication from the European Commission to the European Parliament, the Council, the European Economic and Social Committee and the Committee of the Regions: The CAP towards 2020: Meeting the food, natural resources and territorial challenges of the future (COM 2010 672 final), http://eur-lex.europa.eu/LexUriServ/LexUriServ.do?uri=COM:2010:0672:FIN:en:PDF (accessed 19.12.2011), 16 pp.

EC (European Commission) (2011 a): Factsheet: Modulation. http://ec.europa.eu/agriculture/direct-support/pdf/factsheet-modulation_en.pdf (accessed 30.11.2011)

EC (European Commission) (2011 b): Factsheet: The Single Payment Scheme. http://ec.europa.eu/agriculture/direct-support/pdf/factsheet-single-payment-scheme_en.pdf (accessed 28.11.2011), 3 pp.

EC (European Commission) (2011 c): Factsheet: The Single Area Payment Scheme. http://ec.europa.eu/agriculture/direct-support/pdf/factsheet-single-area-payment-scheme_en.pdf (accessed 28.11.2011), 1 p.

EC (European Commission) (2011 d): Agricultural Policy Perspectives Briefs: The Future of Direct Payments. Brief No. 2, January 2011, http://ec.europa.eu/agriculture/publi/app-briefs/02_en.pdf (accessed 28.11.2011), 9 pp.

EC (European Commission) (2011 e): Factsheet: Specific Support. http://ec.europa.eu/agriculture/direct-support/pdf/factsheet-specific-support_en.pdf (accessed 28.11.2011), 2 pp.

EC (European Commission) (2011 f): Rural Development Policy 2007-2013. http://ec.europa.eu/agriculture/rurdev/index_en.htm (accessed 30.11.2011)

EC (European Commission) (2011 g): The Common Agricultural Policy. Special Eurobarometer 368, Report, http://ec.europa.eu/public_opinion/archives/ebs/ebs_368_en.pdf (accessed 15.12.2011), 65 pp.

EC (European Commission) (2011 h): Proposal for a regulation of the European Parliament and of the Council establishing rules to direct payments to farmers under support schemes within the framework of the common agricultural policy. COM(2011) 625/3, 2011/0280 (COD), http://ec.europa.eu/agriculture/cap-post-2013/legal-proposals/com625/625_en.pdf (accessed 13.10.2011), 105 pp.

EC (European Commission) (2011 i): CAP Reform – an explanation of the main elements. Memo/11/685, 12.10.2011, http://europa.eu/rapid/pressReleasesAction.do?reference=MEMO/11/685&format=HTML&aged=0&language=EN&guiLanguage=en (accessed 12.10.2011)

EC (European Commission) (2011 j): Proposal for a regulation of the European Parliament and of the Council establishing a common organisation of the markets in agricultural products (Single CMO Regulation), draft, http://www.meine-landwirtschaft.de/fileadmin/files/meine-landwirtschaft/CAP_proposal_on_CMOs_07-09-2011_16-24-40.pdf (accessed 13.10.2011), 252 pp.

EC (European Commission) (2011 k): Proposal for a regulation of the European Parliament and of the Council on support for rural development by the European Agricultural Fund for Rural Development (EAFRD). COM(2011) 627/final/2, http://ec.europa.eu/agriculture/cap-post-2013/legal-proposals/com627/627_en.pdf (accessed 30.1.2012), 143 pp.

ECA (European Court of Auditors) (2012): Opinion No 1/2012 on certain proposals for regulations relating to the common agricultural policy for the period 2014-2020. http://eca.europa.eu/portal/pls/portal/docs/1/13768739.PDF (accessed 11.6.2012)

EP (European Parliament) (2011): Reform of the CAP. Focus. http://www.europarl.europa.eu/pdfs/news/public/focus/20110526FCS20313/20110526FCS20313_en.pdf (accessed 30.11.2011), 5 pp.

Erjavec, Karmen; Erjavec, Emil; Juvančič, Luka (2009): New Wine in Old Bottles: Critical Discourse Analysis of the Current Common EU Agricultural Policy Reform Agenda. Sociologia Ruralis, Volume 49, Number 1, pp. 41-55

Hofreither, Markus F. (2011): GAP-Reform 2013 und langfristiger Reformpfad. Agrarische Rundschau 2/2011, pp.8-13

IfLS (Institute for Rural Development Research at Johann Wolfgang Goethe-University), Chair for Economic Development and Integration, Wilhelm Merton Centre for European Integration and International Economic Order at Goethe University Frankfurt/Main (edit.) (2012): Is the Common Agricultural Policy Rising to its Challenges? A European Dialogue. Executive summary of synthesis report and conference proceedings. Frankfurt, 58 pp.

Juvančič, Luka (2012): Synthesis and assessment of the public debate on the reform of the CAP after 2013: Slovenia. Ljubljana, http://www.ifls.de/downloads.html?&L=1, 54 pp.

Lataste, François-Gaël; Trouvé, Aurélie (2011): Synthesis and assessment of the public debate on the reform of the CAP after 2013: France. Dijon, http://www.ifls.de/downloads.html?&L=1, 35 pp.

Liesivaara, Petri; Huan-Niemi, Ellen; Niemi, Jyrki (2011): Synthesis and assessment of the public debate on the reform of the CAP after 2013: Finland. Helsinki, http://www.ifls.de/downloads.html?&L=1, 36 pp.

Meester, Gerrit (2010): European integration and its relevance for agriculture, food and rural areas. In: Oskam, Arie; Meester, Gerrit; Silvis, Huib (editors) (2010): EU policy for agriculture, food and rural areas. Wageningen Academic Publishers, Wageningen, pp. 29-40

Nurzyńska, Iwona (2011): Synthesis and assessment of the public debate on the reform of the CAP after 2013: Poland. Warszawa, http://www.ifls.de/downloads.html?&L=1, 46 pp.

Ocsko, Edina (2011): Synthesis and assessment of the public debate on the reform of the CAP after 2013: Hungary. Budapest, http://www.ifls.de/downloads.html?&L=1, 51 pp.

Prazan, Jaroslav (2011): Synthesis and assessment of the public debate on the reform of the CAP after 2013: The Czech Republic. Brno, http://www.ifls.de/downloads.html?&L=1, 27 pp.

Rutz, Cordula; Dwyer, Janet; Schramek, Jörg (2012): More New Wine in the Same Old Bottles? The evolving nature of the CAP reform debate in Europe, 2010-11, and prospects for the future. Paper at the Agricultural Economics Society annual conference 2012, Warwick, 18 pp.

Rutz, Cordula; Schramek, Jörg; von Urff, Winfried (2011): Synthesis and assessment of the public debate on the reform of the CAP after 2013: Germany. Frankfurt/Main, http://www.ifls.de/downloads.html?&L=1, 46 pp.

Silvis, Huib; Lapperre, Roald (2010): Market, price and quota policy: half a century of CAP experience. In: Oskam, Arie; Meester, Gerrit; Silvis, Huib (editors) (2010): EU policy for agriculture, food and rural areas. Wageningen Academic Publishers, Wageningen, pp.165-182

Swinnen, Jo; Dries, Liesbeth; Negash, Marta; Vandemoortele, Thijs (2010): Consumers and EU agricultural and food policies. In: Oskam, Arie; Meester, Gerrit; Silvis, Huib (editors) (2010): EU policy for agriculture, food and rural areas. Wageningen Academic Publishers, Wageningen, pp.255-265

Swinnen, Johan F.M. (2008) (edit.): The Perfect Storm: the political economy of the Fischler reforms of the Common Agricultural Policy. Centre for European Policy Studies, Brussels, 184 pp.

Thomson, Ken; Berkhout, Petra; Constantinou, Antonis (2010): Balancing between structural and rural policy.. In: Oskam, Arie; Meester, Gerrit; Silvis, Huib (editors) (2010): EU policy for agriculture, food and rural areas. Wageningen Academic Publishers, Wageningen, pp. 377-392

Viladomiu, Lourdes; Rosell, Jordi (2011): Synthesis and assessment of the public debate on the reform of the CAP after 2013: Spain. Barcelona, http://www.ifls.de/downloads.html?&L=1, 59 pp.

Vlahos, George; Klonaris, Stathis (2011): Synthesis and assessment of the public debate on the reform of the CAP after 2013: Greece. Athens, http://www.ifls.de/downloads.html?&L=1, 44 pp.

7. Annex

7.1 Annex 1: Overview of the Implementation of Direct Payments under the CAP in Selected Member States in 2012

Member State	Start date	Model	Separate payments decoupled	Sectors remaining coupled and transitional coupled payments of the fruit and vegetable sector	Specific Support under Articles 68-72
Czech Republic	2004	SAPS	Separate sugar payments 100% Separate payment for tomatoes intended for processing 100%		Aid for dairy farmers, aid for sheep and goat sector, for starch potato sector, Improving quality on hops and suckler cow sectors
Germany	2005	SPS dynamic hybrid moving to a flat rate			
Greece	2006	SPS historical		Cotton	Improvement of quality of olive oil, durum wheat LFA producers in meat sectors (beef, sheep and goat) Restructuring programmes in LFA Mountainous areas
Spain	2006	SPS historical		Suckler cow premium 100%, cotton 35%, sugar	Improving quality of legumes, tobacco, sheep and goat farmers and milk products, beef meat, sugar beet and cotton programme crop rotation non-irrigated land Aid to goat sector in LFA, Support for suckler cows, dairy sector and sheep sector in vulnerable areas

Member State	Start date	Model	Separate payments decoupled	Sectors remaining coupled and transitional coupled payments of the fruit and vegetable sector	Specific Support under Articles 68-72
France	2006	SPS historical		Suckler cow premium 75%, F&V: until end 2012: 75% of national envelope for orchards producing prunes, peaches and pears intended for processing	Additional aid for protein crops, Aid for quality of durum wheat, To maintain organic farming, For conversion to organic farming, Aid for calves from suckling cows and for organic labelled calves, aid for sheep and goat producers, aid for milk producers in mountain areas, Fattening of young calves Crop harvest insurance, Mutual funds in case of animal or vegetal diseases or environmental incidents
Hungary	2004	SAPS	Separate sugar payments 100% Separate F&V payments for tomatoes and other fruits 100%, separate soft fruit payment 100%		Dairy sector, rice sector For tobacco, fresh fruit and vegetables growing areas, bovine sector and ovine sector subject to restructuring and development programmes
Poland	2004	SAPS	Separate sugar payments 100% Separate F&V payment for tomatoes 100% Separate soft fruit payment 100%		For cultivating pulses and herbage legumes Improving the quality in the tobacco sector For keeping cows in South-Eastern Poland and sheep in Southern Poland
Slovenia	2007	SPS regional			For extensive rearing of female bovine animals and dairy payment for farmers in mountain areas and on steep hills, Preserving animal rearing on farms with permanent pastures

Member State	Start date	Model	Separate payments decoupled	Sectors remaining coupled and transitional coupled payments of the fruit and vegetable sector	Specific Support under Articles 68-72
Finland	2006	SPS dynamic hybrid moving to a flat rate		Sheep and goat premium 50	Supporting protein, oilseed and starch potato crops, Quality premium for slaughtered lambs, Supporting beef and veal production, dairy cow premium
United Kingdom	2005	England: SPS dynamic hybrid moving to a flat rate Scotland: SPS historical Wales: SPS historical Northern Ireland: SPS static hybrid			Scottish beef scheme

Source: Adapted from European Commission, Directorate General for Agriculture and Rural Development, January 2012 http://ec.europa.eu/agriculture/direct-support/pdf/implementation-direct-payments_en.pdf (accessed 13.2.2012), 4pp.

7.2 Annex 2: Tabular Overview of Stakeholders' Positions

The reader should be aware that the following tables do not reflect all the differences between the positions within and between stakeholder groups, but provide a broad overview.

Challenges and targets

Nearly all stakeholders agree with the challenges and targets stated by the Commission. In particular the following issues were emphasised:

SH	MS	
G	CZ	Competitiveness, more equal distribution among MS, simplification
	FI	To maintain agriculture in the entire EU, simplification
	FR	Various, including: Sufficient incomes for farmers, increased production capacity, to create employment, focus on internal consumption rather than exports, to support legumes
	DE	Competitiveness and environmental issues, simplification
	EL	Maintain agriculture in the entire EU, balanced territorial development
	HU	Simplification, more efficient delivery, Parliamentary Commissioner for Future Generations: conflict between sustainability and growth
	PL	Growth oriented competitiveness, contribution to meet global food demand, simplification
	SI	Funds are insufficient to achieve objectives
	ES	To ensure sufficient income for farmers
	UK	Central Government: Shift from sectoral policy support to public support for the provision of public goods, proposals fall short of challenges
F	CZ	Competitiveness and productivity
	FI	To maintain agriculture in the entire EU, income support for farmers
	FR	Competitiveness and productivity, adequate funding, innovations
	DE	Competitiveness and productivity, full implementation of previous reforms
	EL	Creation of wealth, competitiveness, food security, employment, reduction of inequalities

SH	MS	
	HU	Support of young farmers, to improve competitiveness, to support animal husbandry
	PL	Global food security, competitiveness, equal support to all farmers
	SI	Equal access to financial resources, stable prices, food security, farm incomes
	ES	Maintenance of viable farms, contribution to global food security
	UK	Competitiveness and productivity, proposals fall short of challenges
S	FI	Payments to be based on objective criteria
	FR	Fundamental reform focusing on market failures, ethical and cohesion objectives; transformation of the CAP into a Common Food Policy
	DE	Policy proposals inadequate to challenges, shift from income policy to integration of EU agriculture into word markets
	HU	Competitiveness, food safety, small farms, poverty reduction
	ES	Fundamental reform, shift from stable income to risk management
N	FI	Environment, climate change, and animal welfare
	FR	Fundamental reform to legitimate the CAP, support for legumes, food sovereignty, rural development, environmental protection, climate change
	DE	Focus on environment and social justice regionally, nationally and internationally
	HU	Public money for public goods
	PL	Fundamental reform promoting sustainable agriculture, small family farms
	SI	Sustainable management of natural resources, biodiversity, fair prices, rural heritage, small farms
	ES	Biodiversity, vitality of rural areas, multifunctionality
	UK	Biodiversity, cultural landscape, climate change mitigation, animal welfare

SH= Stakeholder, MS=Member States

G=Governmental & administrative bodies, F= Farmers organisations& food related industry
S=Scientific advisory boards & individual scientists, N=NGOs

Reform orientation

The main issues under this heading are a more equal distribution of funds between Member States and the maintenance of the two pillar structure. The following table provides the position of Member States on these issues and additional topics raised.

SH	MS	
G	CZ	More equity endorsed, transition period to be shortened, two pillar structure agreed, no increase in national co-financing
	FI	More equity endorsed, continuation of two pillar structure
	FR	More equity accepted but situation of the national agricultural sector contribution to EU budget should be taken into account. Structural changes suggested by some stakeholders (e.g. one pillar with three components suggested by Ministry of the Environment).
	DE	Equity opposed (only minor redistribution accepted), two pillar structure as in the past agreed
	EL	More solidarity demanded, shift from historical to regional model reduces inequality,, structural characteristics to be taken into account, to support small farms
	HU	More equity endorsed, structure not questioned
	PL	More equity endorsed, two pillar structure agreed
	SI	More equity accepted but existing allocation also to be taken into account
	ES	Distribution to be based on objective criteria, two pillar structure agreed
	UK	Central Government: First pillar to be phased out and second pillar to be strengthened Devolved Administrations: Need for adequate funding
F	CZ	More equity endorsed, fast implementation, attempts to co-financing rejected
	FI	Different production environments to be taken into account
	FR	Equity opposed (with the exception of one organisation)
	DE	Equity opposed, differences in purchasing power and costs to be taken into account
	HU	More equity endorsed, two pillar structure agreed, first pillar not to be weakened
	PL	More equity endorsed, two pillar structure agreed, no renationalisation

SH	MS	
	ES	Equity opposed, Spain suffering from climate change, two pillar structure agreed but agro-environment measures in pillar one and rural development part of cohesion policy
	UK	Equity issue controversial among farmers organisations
S	FI	More equity endorsed
	FR	All measures to be co-financed from national budgets. One pillar preferred with three components: basic income support, payments for environmental services and contractual payments for agro-ecological transition
	DE	Commission proposals inappropriate
	HU	More equity endorsed, three pillars (markets, rural development, agro-environment) or two additional pillars (risk management, social food policy) proposed
	PL	Budget allocations to be based on fair and objective criteria
	ES	Decrease of EU budget, more nationally co-financed measures, three pillar structure
N	FR	One pillar scheme proposed by environmental organisations
	PL	First pillar to include flat rate payments, support for less-favoured areas, environmental payments as well as other targeted payments. National direct payment levels should range between 80 and 120% of the EU average.
	SI	One single pillar
	ES	Many different proposals such as two pillars with agro environment measures in pillar one and rural development as part of cohesion policy, one pillar with five axes (basic farm and market support, innovation, information and investment, agro environment, diversification, LEADER approach)

SH= Stakeholder, MS=Member States

G=Governmental & administrative bodies, F= Farmers organisations& food related industry

S=Scientific advisory boards & individual scientists, N=NGOs

Direct payments

This table provides an overview of the positions on the proposed capping of direct payments and the limitation to "active farmers".

SH	MS	Capping	Limitation to "active farmers"[6]
G	CZ	No, impair competitiveness, increase bureaucracy	Undecided
	FI	Of minor importance for the country	Yes
	FR	Min. of. Agriculture: no position taken. Others: to be based on employment	Yes
	DE	Not justified for remuneration for public goods, impair competitiveness, increase bureaucracy	No, part time farmers
	EL	Yes, lower limit suggested	Sceptical, should be left to MS
	HU	Yes if remaining funds used according to national priorities	No, part time f.
	PL	Principally welcomed, fear of increased bureaucracy	No
	SI	No position taken	No
	ES	No uniform position	Yes, different concepts suggested
	UK	Central government: No, direct payments to be passed out anyway, negative impact on efficiency	National decision
F	CZ	No, discrimination of large farms, impair competitiveness	Yes
	FI	Of minor importance for the country	
	FR	No uniform position	
	DE	No, negative impact on efficiency	No
	EL	Yes	Yes
	HU	No, negative impact on efficiency, young farmers are in favour	Yes

6 Most stakeholders who accepted the restriction on active farmers criticized the definition proposed by the Commission.

SH	MS	Capping	Limitation to "active farmers"[6]
	PL	No position taken	
	SI	No position taken	Yes
	ES	Coupling to employment accepted but young farmers critical	Yes
	UK	No, impair structural change	No
S	CZ	Only a small number of farms affected	
	DE	No, only relation to income criteria may be justified	No
	ES	Direct payments to be abolished	
N	FI	Supported by animal welfare organisations	Different posit.
	FR	Yes and coupling to employment	
	DE	Yes and coupling to employment	Yes
	PL	Yes	Yes
	ES	Yes	Different positions

SH= Stakeholder, MS=Member States

G=Governmental & administrative bodies, F= Farmers organisations& food related industry

S=Scientific advisory boards & individual scientists, N=NGOs

6 Most stakeholders who accepted the restriction on active farmers criticized the definition proposed by the Commission.

Direct payments

This table provides an overview of the positions on the proposed greening, support to farmers suffering from specific constraints, small farmers, young farmers, partially coupled support.

SH	MS	Greening	Special support
G	CZ	Principally welcomed, but design criticised	
	FI	Specifications too rigid, too much bureaucracy	Coupled payments
	FR	Min. of Agriculture: Yes if farmers' economic situation is taken into account, specifications too rigid. Min. of Environment: Stricter obligations	Coupled payments
	DE	To be taken into account by the second pillar	
	EL	No, additional burden on farmers	Small farms, specific constraints
	HU	Principally accepted, but fear of additional burden on farmers, additional costs	Small farms, young farmers, coupled payments
	PL	No, additional burden on farmers, additional costs	Small farms
	SI	Accepted but specifications to be left to MS taking specific conditions into account	Small farms, young farmers, spec. constraints
	ES	No, additional burden on farmers, additional costs, impair competitiveness	Maintain distinction betw. P 1 & P 2, coupled payments
	UK	No, impact questioned	
F	CZ	No, impair competitiveness and productivity	
	FI	No, impair competitiveness and productivity	Coupled payments
	FR	No, impair competitiveness but small farmers agree	
	DE	No, impair competitiveness and productivity	
	EL	Rejected because of too rigid specifications	
	HU	No, impair competitiveness and productivity	

SH	MS	Greening	Special support
	PL	Not necessary because of existing cross-compliance	
	SI	Too rigid specifications with regard to ecological areas, administrative burden	Specific constr., young f.
	ES	No, impair competitiveness and productivity	Coupled payments
	UK	No, impair competitiveness and productivity	
S	FI	Objective criteria for public goods to be taken into account	
	DE	No, impact questioned, subject of the second pillar	
	HU	Uniform flat rate based on cross-compliance, simplified administration	Part of nat. envelope to Support spec. industries
	PL	No, additional complication	More for small farmers
	ES	Direct payments to be abolished, move towards contractual pay.	
N	CZ	Obligations insufficient, appropriate measures should be compulsory for all MS and all farm sizes	
	FI	Obligations insufficient, more on animal welfare	
	FR	Obligations insufficient	
	DE	Obligations insufficient even counterproductive	
	HU	Obligations insufficient	
	PL	Proposal welcomed	
	SI	Amendments proposed: small & organic farms, grassland	
	ES	Strongly supported, amendments proposed, after transition period regional model to be replaced by contractual payments	
	UK	Obligations insufficient,payments to be targeted to the delivery of public goods & services	

SH= Stakeholder, MS=Member States

G=Governmental & administrative bodies, F= Farmers organisations& food related industry

S=Scientific advisory boards & individual scientists, N=NGOs

Market Measures

This table provides an overview on the positions on market instruments, the strengthening of producers in the food supply chain, risk management, quality policy and further issues raised.

SH	MS	
G	CZ	Risk & crisis management tools in addition to existing safety net measures
	FI	Strengthening producers welcomed, to maintain sugar quota system
	FR	Supply management tools, risk management tools, counter cyclical subsidies, stricter rules on imports
	DE	Strengthening producers welcomed, quality production, labelling, risk management tools, export subsidies to be abolished under WTO rules
	EL	Existing measures plus risk management tools
	HU	To maintain sugar quotas, suspension of wine planting rights opposed
	PL	To maintain present intervention system, risk management tools, promotion activities to be strengthened
	SI	To maintain present intervention system and wine planting rights, to abolish sugar quotas, risk management tools, interbranch organisations
	ES	To strengthen present intervention system and support producers & interbranch organisations risk management tools, EU standards for imports
	UK	To simplify the system, abolish export subsidies & quota systems, temporary support to private risk management tools
F	CZ	Strengthening producers welcomed, risk management tools
	FI	Strengthening producers welcomed, risk management tools (for producer groups), maintain sugar quotas and export subsidies
	FR	Strong market interventions, supply management tools, maintain quota systems
	DE	Strengthening producers welcomed, maintain sugar & wine market organisations
	EL	To maintain or strengthen present system including export subsidies
	HU	Strengthening producers welcomed

SH	MS	
	PL	More instruments to protect farm incomes, more efforts to strengthen producers
	ES	To maintain present system including quota systems, more efforts to strengthen producers, support to risk management tools
	UK	Strengthening producers by regulating contractual terms for the food sector
S	FR	Intervention to be reduced to safety nets, temporary support to private risk management tools
	DE	To abolish quota systems & export subsidies, temporary support to private risk management tools
	ES	To abolish quota systems & wine planting ban, improve quality production
N	FR	To abolish export subsidies, environmental standards for imports, support for local food markets
	DE	No support to risk management tools, abolish export subsidies (even export ban on products benefiting from direct payments), no abolition of sugar quotas
	PL	To strengthen connection between producers and consumers through local food chains
	ES	To support local food chains, as well as labelling and traceability systems, stricter rules on imports

SH= Stakeholder, MS=Member States

G=Governmental & administrative bodies, F= Farmers organisations& food related industry
S=Scientific advisory boards & individual scientists, N=NGOs

Rural Development

This table provides an overview of the positions on criteria used for the distribution of funds, the focus of the second pillar and further issues raised.

SH	MS	
G	CZ	Funds to be distributed on objective criteria (depopulation, unemployment), partner agreements seen with suspicion
	FI	Compensatory payments based on biophysical criteria for agri-environmental programmes & climatic criteria for LFA programmes welcomed, inclusion of Baltic Sea Strategy objectives in agri-environmental programmes demanded, better harmonisation between EU funds
	FR	RDP does not receive much attention, more decision power to be transferred to the regional level
	DE	Compensatory payments based on biophysical & climatic criteria questioned, stronger incentives for participation in agri-environmental measures
	PL	Importance for the catching-up process of new MS, pillar 2 – LEADER approach in particular – to be strengthened, improved targeting
	SI	Priorities agreed, strategic framework supported
	ES	Priority to be given to competitiveness, implementation in the form of territorial contracts suggested by some stakeholders
	UK	Targeted to provision of public goods, better co-ordination between EU funds, LEADER approach to be strengthened
F	FI	Maintain current structure of second pillar.
	DE	Stronger focus on competitiveness, re-introduction of incentive component in agri-environmental measures
	EL	Stronger focus on agriculture
	HU	Important, but no transfer from pillar 1 into pillar 2
	PL	Redefinition of LFA based on objective criteria, importance for modernisation of agro food sector
	SI	Proposals welcomed, focus on knowledge transfer to agriculture and forestry
	ES	Priority to be given to competitiveness, rural diversification to be excluded from CAP
S	FI	Compensatory payments based on biophysical & climatic criteria welcomed, better target orientation
	FR	Bottom-up integrative projects preferred

SH	MS	
	DE	Truly multisectoral approaches preferred
	HU	Better coordination between rural development measures and cohesion policy, emphasis on poverty reduction
N	CZ	To increase budget for pillar 2
	FI	Compensatory payments based on biophysical & climatic criteria welcomed, more target orientation
	FR	50 % of pillar 2 funds to be spent on environment protection
	DE	Strengthening of pillar 2, focus on integrated rural development, environment, animal welfare and organic farming, greater variety of measures
	HU	Devolution of competences and resources, LEADER approach to be strengthened
	PL	Focus on strategic goals at EU level, MS and regions should be responsible for establishing strategic rural development frameworks combining urban and rural areas, LEADER approach to be strengthened
	SI	Concerns over some proposed changes because of conflicts between competitiveness and environmental benefits and lack of proposals how to evaluate how to measure progress towards environmental priorities, better coordination of rural development policies
	ES	Sustainability and public goods seen as most important aims of rural development policy
	UK	Removal of minimum spending on former axis 2 of pillar 2 and introduction of risk management criticised

SH= Stakeholder, MS=Member States

G=Governmental & administrative bodies, F= Farmers organisations& food related industry
S=Scientific advisory boards & individual scientists, N=NGOs